Sir Andrew Aguecheek

Malvolio

Feste

Favourite Tales from
Shakespeare
Bernard Miles

illustrated by
Victor G. Ambrus

Hamlyn
London · New York · Sydney · Toronto

For
Anna, Ben, Mary Ann, Josephine, Jack major,
John, Jack minor, Dido and Hannah,
with love from Grampie

First published 1976
Third impression 1978 by
The Hamlyn Publishing Group Limited
London · New York · Sydney · Toronto
Astronaut House, Hounslow Road, Feltham, Middlesex, England
© Copyright 1976 The Hamlyn Publishing Group Limited

ISBN 0 600 38019 X

Printed and bound in Spain
by Graficromo, S. A. – Córdoba

Contents

Bottom

Introduction

This is a family book. Parents can read it to children, children can read it to parents, parents and children can read it to each other or to themselves and perhaps, most important of all, tiny children can enjoy the pictures. Mothers can give them drawing paper and paints and let them pin down their own infant visions of ships tossed to and fro by storms, of girls dressed up as boys, of ghosts walking on castle walls, of witches weaving their spells, of elves and goblins living out their lives deep in magic woodlands.

Shakespeare's plays are mostly made of poetry and they were written nearly four hundred years ago, so they aren't always easy to understand. Also the plays only give you what people *say* to each other. They don't tell you what they look like or how they dress or what kind of house they live in. We don't know how they get from place to place or what has been happening to them between the time you saw them last and the next time they appear – only pages and pages of talk in beautiful but rather difficult and old-fashioned language.

And yet, locked away inside the plays are some of the most exciting stories ever told; some romantic, some tragic, some comic, but all full of interesting people doing very much the sort of things people do today – getting into difficulties and trying to get out of them, turning up late for appointments, mistaking one person for another and so on.

One of the best ways to learn about these magnificent plays is to get someone to tell you the stories hidden away inside them, the frameworks or skeletons that the poetry and the people who speak it are fastened to. Shakespeare himself always took other people's stories for his plays, some from a very old English book called the Anglo-Saxon Chronicle, some from a famous history book written by a man named Tom Holinshed, some from a book about the Romans by a writer named Plutarch, and some from Spanish or Italian books which had only recently been translated into English.

So in this book I have taken five of his most exciting plays and tried to turn them back into the kind of stories he started out with. I haven't always followed the plays exactly and here and there I have even added a little from my imagination, but only the sort of things I believe Shakespeare would have allowed me to say if he had been sitting beside me! He often altered the stories to suit the play and he put in fresh scenes and extra people, so I don't think he would object to the little bits I have added here and there!

Shakespeare was an actor as well as a play-writer, and although in his time London was not much bigger than a small market town and had only three or four proper theatres, people

William Shakespeare

flocked to see the exciting plays that he and his fellow poets were writing and putting on the stage. And the people who built and managed the theatres were always wanting new plays and were willing to pay for them. So Shakespeare was kept very busy and at last he became a manager himself and grew quite rich and after working for twenty-five years in London he went back to his birthplace, Stratford on Avon, to write one or two more plays before he died.

The theatres in which his plays were first performed were big open-air enclosures with galleries all round and a great platform thrusting out into the middle. Some of them held as many as two thousand people, many of them standing pressed right up against the stage itself, others even sitting on it. The audiences were very noisy and even quarrelsome, but there was plenty of music and cannon-fire and beating of drums and dancing and sword-fighting and clowning and, riding over it all, the voices of the actors, ringing clear, speaking the wonderful words of the greatest play-writer the world has ever seen.

The theatre in which most of Shakespeare's plays were performed was called the Globe. It stood close to the South Bank of the River Thames, opposite St Paul's Cathedral. But Shakespeare himself lived on the North Bank, in the City of London, and during much of his working life he was one of the owners and managers of a small theatre in Blackfriars, only a few yards from where the famous Mermaid Theatre now stands. So if you come to the Mermaid, you will be standing on ground which many great theatre-folk have trodden, including Shakespeare and Ben Jonson, John Marston and Philip Massinger, Francis Beaumont and John Fletcher and many others – also many of the lucky performers who acted in their famous plays for the very first time.

At first I tried turning some of the speeches from the plays into the everyday English we speak today. But the words Shakespeare uses and the magical way he joins them together cannot be copied. So in the end I thought it best to tell the stories as plainly as possible, then with a superb artist, make them into a picture book. And I was very lucky to meet Victor Ambrus and very happy to find that he loves Shakespeare as much as I do.

For the most thrilling of all theatres is inside our own heads. It's called Imagination. And when you read this book and look at the beautiful pictures I hope the stories will come alive just as vividly as if you were watching them being performed by live actors in a real theatre, and that they will lead you to love Shakespeare and all the wonderful characters he created for the rest of your lives.

Bernard Miles

9

Macbeth

LONG, long ago, three witches lived on a lonely moorland away out in the highlands of Scotland. Perhaps they are still there. I don't know. If ever you go there, keep a sharp look-out, especially when the weather is dark and stormy.

Day and night, these witches boiled up wicked thoughts in a cauldron and danced round it hand-in-hand, lying in wait for people they could tempt, lives they could ruin. They could not tempt good people, only people whose thoughts were already evil.

Their spells were very powerful. They could look into people's minds and read them. If people were only a tiny bit wicked, the witches could make them wickeder still. They lived in a cave, and they made their temptations by boiling up horrible things like bits of toads and frogs and newts and lizards and snakes, or things taken from the stomachs of dead sharks – all the nastiest things you could possibly think of. They kept their cauldron always on the boil, and they could fly through the air to any place they liked, screaming on the wind and carrying their magic fire already lit, and singing an ugly little song:

'Fair is foul and foul is fair,
Hover through the fog and filthy air!'

They were not like witches you read about in fairy tales, but deadly and dangerous ones.

At this time Scotland was divided into small areas like counties, each ruled by a lord called a thane, and these thanes had to obey the king and help him whenever he was in danger. And if they did it well, he rewarded them with more land and with high titles and kept them close to him because he could trust them and rely on them.

In the long-time-ago of our story the King was Duncan. He was old and silver-haired, generous and wise and good, and he had two sons, Malcolm and Donalbain; and when he died Malcolm would be king. And all the thanes would swear to serve him just as faithfully as they had served Duncan.

But one of the thanes, named Macbeth, thought that when Duncan died, he and not Malcolm had a right to be king. And his wife, Lady Macbeth, thought the same. In fact she kept talking about it, until he really began to believe it.

Of course it wasn't possible while Duncan and his sons were still alive. But who knows, the chance might come. Some accident might befall them! At all events, the thought was there inside Macbeth's head and if ever he should meet the witches he was just the sort of person they could fasten upon, someone whose mind was ready to receive and act upon the wicked thoughts they were brewing out there in the fog and filthy air of the moor.

King Duncan

Banquo

Macbeth

14

And then, in a quite unexpected way, the chance did come. The King of Norway came across the sea and attacked Scotland, and the Thane of Cawdor and some of the other thanes turned traitor and joined him. So Duncan called together all the thanes who were faithful to him and told them to bring their soldiers and help him. And there was a mighty battle between the two sides. And the bravest on Duncan's side was Macbeth. Along with his friend Banquo he fought so hard and killed so many of the enemy that at last they gained the victory and the King of Norway and the Thane of Cawdor were both driven from the battlefield. Macbeth was very proud to have beaten the King's enemies and he set off with Banquo to tell the King all about the battle, then return to his beloved wife at Glamis Castle, which was their home.

But the way lay across the wild and lonely moorland, and as they rode through the mist, weary and blood-stained, night came down with thunder and lightning, and with the night the thought came back to Macbeth that somehow, by some means, he must become king, and he could not get it out of his mind. He felt he had served his country so well that it was no more than he deserved. And how wonderful it would be if Fate could make it happen! How his wife would enjoy it and what a beautiful queen she would make! So Macbeth and Banquo rode on over the moor.

Suddenly there came a flash of lightning and there were the three witches right in their path, their ugly faces lit by the glow from their magic fire. Macbeth and Banquo reined in their horses sharply, almost riding the witches down. And you can imagine how surprised they were when the three old hags hailed them. It seemed they knew who Macbeth was, for they called him Thane of Glamis. Then they told him he would soon be Thane of Cawdor as well and that one day he would even be king! How strange that these three ugly old women crouched over their cauldron on the wild moorland, should know what had been going on inside his mind!

Then the witches spoke to Banquo, telling him that even though he would never be king himself, his children would be, and his grandchildren and his great grandchildren, on and on for hundreds of years.

Macbeth commanded the witches to tell them more. He asked them how they were able to look into the future and see things that had not yet happened. How did they come by this strange knowledge? But the witches would not be commanded. There came another lightning flash and they melted away into the air and the moorland was empty again, except for the thunder and lightning and the swirling mist and the howling wind.

Macbeth was astonished that the witches should know his name and title and even more astonished to be told that he would soon be Thane of Cawdor, for the Thane of Cawdor had not been killed in the battle. He had escaped and was still alive. But most of all he was deeply disturbed that someone should tell him that one day he would be king, for apart from his wife he had never spoken of this to a soul.

He was also astonished when the witches prophesied that Banquo, not himself, would be father to a whole line of kings. But for the moment he thought mostly of himself, and his heart pounded with excitement and he longed to get home and tell his wife what the witches had promised.

He and Banquo had just mounted their horses and were about to start off again through the storm when messengers came riding up to tell them that the King had heard of Macbeth's bravery in the battle and had created him Thane of Cawdor as a reward.

'But how can that be?' said Macbeth. 'The Thane of Cawdor is still alive. I saw him escape from the battle.'

The messengers replied that the Thane of Cawdor had been captured and because of his treachery had been stripped of his title. Now he was under sentence of death and Duncan had given his title to Macbeth, just as the witches had prophesied.

Lady Macbeth

King Duncan

18

At this news Macbeth's heart began to beat faster still. If the witches could see into the future like this, if they knew that he had already been created Thane of Cawdor, might not their other prophecy also come true, that one day he would come to be king? At this thought he found it hard to control his excitement. Surely the witches, and the supernatural powers that guided them, were working on his side!

When at last they came to Duncan, the old King greeted them lovingly and shed tears of gratitude, for they had saved him and his kingdom by their bravery. He clasped them both to his heart and told Macbeth that he would come that very evening to stay at Glamis Castle, to honour him and show how highly he prized him. His sons Malcolm and Donalbain would come as well, along with other thanes and members of the Court, and they would hold a great feast to celebrate the victory. And, of course, Banquo must be there too, for he had fought almost as bravely as Macbeth.

So Macbeth hurried home to break the news to his wife and to get the castle ready for the King's visit, to prepare a room for him and the two guards who always slept beside his bedroom door, and to make ready the food and wine for the feast.

When he arrived he found that his wife had already heard of the victory and of how the King had rewarded him for his bravery. But when she heard that Duncan was coming to stay with them she could hardly contain herself, for she realised that this was the chance she had been secretly dreaming of, the chance to kill him and so make way for her and her husband to become king and queen.

When she told Macbeth what was in her mind he was shocked and said they must never commit such a terrible crime. But she came close to him and pressed her beautiful body against his and whispered fiercely in his ear that if they let this opportunity slip the chance might never come again. Macbeth said: 'Yes, but what if we fail?' She told him not to talk of failing. If they both screwed their courage up tightly enough they could not possibly fail. So at last Macbeth agreed. They would drug the King's guards and wait till he was fast asleep, then Macbeth would steal quietly into the bedroom and murder him.

When Duncan and his courtiers arrived, Lady Macbeth put on her most friendly face to welcome them and the old King took her in his arms and kissed her, saying what a beautiful home she had and how fresh and sweet the air felt up there in the mountains and how lovely it was to see the birds nesting in the shelter of the castle walls, and how much he had been looking forward to his visit.

That night at the feast the King praised him so highly that Macbeth was ashamed of what he and his wife were planning to do. He took her out into the courtyard and told her that the King had showered so many honours on him since the battle that he could not dream of killing him. But Lady Macbeth taunted him and called him a coward, saying that if he would not do the murder, she would. So at last Macbeth agreed to go through with the terrible plan. Then together they went back into the castle.

When the feast was over and everyone had gone to bed Macbeth came out into the courtyard again to breathe the cool air and quieten his nerves, for the more he thought about murdering someone as old and innocent and generous as Duncan the more terrified he became, and he imagined the angels of heaven crying out in horror and calling to God to stop him doing it. Then he suddenly thought he could see a blood-stained dagger hanging in the air and pointing to the stairway which led to Duncan's bedroom. That frightened him even more, and though it was a cold night the sweat poured down his face and he trembled.

It was really one of the witches who had hung the dagger in the air, masking her face with her ragged sleeve as she offered Macbeth the handle. They now had him completely in their power and knew all that was going on in his mind and, although no-one saw them, they were hovering above the courtyard watching him and quietly laughing to themselves because their wicked spells were working out so well.

At last Lady Macbeth came out to join her husband and to add her courage to his. She told him that she had drugged the two guards and that the old King was now fast asleep. She would slip back into the hall and when she was sure the coast was clear she would strike on the castle bell and that would be the signal for Macbeth to steal silently up the winding stone stairway into Duncan's bedroom where he would turn down the golden coverlet and plunge his dagger into the old King's heart.

As she went back into the castle, leaving Macbeth alone with his fears, Banquo and his son Fleance came out into the courtyard, and Banquo reminded Macbeth of their meeting with the witches out on the moors. He wondered if the promise they had made to him would come as true as the one they had made to Macbeth, and when Macbeth could spare the time he would like to talk further about these mysterious happenings.

Although he was very frightened at the thought of the awful deed he was about to do, Macbeth said he would gladly find a time for them to meet and talk together. So Banquo and Fleance went back into the castle while Macbeth paced the courtyard, praying that when the time came to go to Duncan's room his footsteps would be so quiet that even the stones would hardly know he was treading on them.

Macbeth

Suddenly the bell struck, loud and clear. The fatal moment had come. Macbeth gathered up his courage and started to walk up the stairs. As he did so Lady Macbeth came out of the castle to wait for him. She was just as frightened as he was but she was harder and more cruel and better able to control her fears.

Although he was gone only a little while it seemed ages as she waited in the shadows of the courtyard. She had taken the two daggers from Duncan's sleeping guards and laid them ready so that Macbeth could not possibly miss them. All the same she dreaded that his courage might fail him when it came to using them. Why oh why was he so long?

All this time the witches were watching, laughing quietly and making little noises to frighten her; the sound of crickets chirping and the hooting of owls and the beating of their wings. They had worked hard for this moment and they were overjoyed that everything was turning out just as they had planned.

At last Macbeth came staggering down the stairway, clutching the two daggers, trembling with fear and ghastly white, his hands soaked with Duncan's blood. Yes, he had done the deed. Stepping over the sleeping bodies of the two guards he had stolen into the King's bedroom, turned down the golden coverlet and plunged the daggers into Duncan's heart just as his wife had bidden him, and Duncan had made a great sigh as the life came out of him and the blood had run in rivers down his silver skin, and poured out onto Macbeth's hands. Then he had stabbed the two guards and they also were dead.

And now he was clinging to his wife, terrified at the awful thing he had done, wishing with all his heart and soul that he had never done it, that he had never listened to the witches or to his wife; that he could be innocent again and go on serving the King as a true and loyal servant. But now it was too late. The deed was done. He was a prisoner and must follow his wickedness to the end.

Lady Macbeth asked him about the two guards. Did they waken or make any sound before he killed them? 'Yes' said Macbeth. 'One of them stirred and murmured a prayer and the other said "Amen". I also tried to say it but the sacred word stuck in my throat.' And this terrifies him, for if he can never pray again or say 'Amen' it will mean that he is cut off from all goodness for ever and ever.

But there was something which terrified him even more. A voice had screamed out in the darkness telling him that what he had done was every bit as wicked as murdering sleep itself and that as a punishment he should never sleep again. And even if he did, his sleep would be shaken by terrible dreams.

It was really one of the witches who had screamed. She had followed him up the stairway to make sure his nerve did not fail

Macbeth

King Duncan

23

him at the last moment and had crouched in the doorway until the deed was done. Only then did she tell Macbeth what the punishment was to be, both for him and his wife. The memory of Duncan lying dead, and the great pools of blood, would stay with them to the very end and help to drive them to their deaths.

But now Lady Macbeth realised that instead of leaving the bloodstained daggers in the bedroom her husband was still clutching them. She seized them boldly, telling him that she herself would return to the scene of the murder and smear some of the blood on the faces of the two guards, then leave the daggers lying beside them so that everyone would believe that they were the real murderers. They had killed the King and then each other in a drunken brawl.

'Go quickly,' she said, 'wash the blood from your hands, then undress and go to our bedroom so that when the murder is discovered we can seem to be innocent.' Then she carried the daggers back to Duncan's bedroom, while Macbeth stood trembling in the courtyard. And all the time the witches were weaving their web of evil tighter round their victims, and happy to see that their plot was working out so well.

Suddenly there came a loud knocking at the castle gate, as if the Day of Judgement had come and the dead were being wakened from their graves. Two of Duncan's most faithful thanes, Macduff and Lennox, had come to greet the King at first daylight and had ridden all night to be with him in good time.

When he heard the knocking Macbeth's heart began once more to pound with terror and he went swiftly into the castle to wash the blood from his hands and quieten his nerves.

The knocking went on for a long time, for the hall porter had been drinking with all the others and was fast asleep. At last he came out and lifted the great bar from the gate to let Macduff and Lennox in. Then Macbeth himself came out. He had cleaned the blood from his hands and thrown a robe over his shoulders and was doing his best to pretend that he was his normal self. Macduff said he would like to go to the King's room, so Macbeth offered to show him the way. But Macduff preferred to go alone, he needed no guide.

For a few moments Lennox stood talking to Macbeth. As they rode through the night both he and Macduff had heard strange noises in the air, lamentings and screams of death and people crying out in fear. And it seemed that the very earth was shaking beneath them. Macbeth agreed that it had been a tough night, otherwise he pretended to be quite unconcerned. But you can imagine how he felt when Macduff came thundering down from the King's room, screaming with horror. He had just seen the old King and his two guards lying dead. He had seen the two daggers and the great pools of blood.

His shouts roused the whole castle and the guests, including Banquo and Duncan's two sons, Malcolm and Donalbain, came pouring out into the courtyard horrified at what they heard and fearful that their own lives might be in danger.

Macbeth's nerves were now close to breaking point. After all he was the host and the safety of the guests was his responsibility. All eyes were turned on him, seeking an answer to the question that was in all their minds. Whoever could have done this terrible deed? Macbeth would have broken down but for his wife's presence of mind.

Realising that her husband was beginning to lose his nerve and that if he broke down he would probably give himself away, she suddenly pretended to faint and fell to the ground. This distracted everyone's attention from Macbeth and gave him time to pull himself together. With a great effort he mastered his fear and suggested that his frightened guests should arm themselves in case of further danger and meet in the castle hall to discuss what should be done next.

But Malcolm and Donalbain, suspecting that whoever had murdered Duncan might soon try to murder them, slipped away into the night and rode across the border into England.

There they separated, Malcolm riding on southwards, Donal-bain turning west to seek safety in Ireland. Banquo also was deeply troubled, for he began to suspect where the guilt for the murder really lay, and he feared, not only for himself, but for his young son Fleance. But for the moment he held his peace and followed the others into the hall.

Now that Malcolm and Donalbain had fled Macbeth claimed the crown and he was so fierce and so strong that his fellow thanes did not dare to oppose him. Indeed they joined in his coronation and agreed to serve him as faithfully as they had formerly served Duncan. So now he was king as the witches had foretold. Their prophecy made on that night of wind and storm following the battle had come true.

Having got his heart's desire you would think Macbeth would now be happy. But he could not rest content, for he remembered how the witches had promised that Banquo would be father to a whole line of kings, and the thought of this burned inside him and led him to commit his second crime.

He invited all the thanes to a feast like the one he gave the night he murdered Duncan. And among the guests would be Banquo and his son Fleance. Indeed Banquo must be the guest of honour and sit next to Lady Macbeth, to show how much he was loved and admired. The invitation to Banquo and Fleance was really a trick, for Macbeth had hired two murderers to lie in wait for them as they rode through the darkness and stab them as they passed.

But the witches knew all he was thinking and spoiled his wicked plan. They also were waiting beside the track where Banquo and Fleance must ride and when the murderers sprang out with their daggers drawn, one of the witches seized Fleance and dragged him away just as the dagger was slashing at his throat. So only Banquo was stabbed and Fleance escaped. And now, to crown their mischief, they led Banquo's ghost, still dripping with blood, to join the guests at the feast. Indeed they took some of the blood from his wounds and while the guests were gathering, glided unseen into the hall and smeared it on the arms of Banquo's chair.

The trumpeters had blown a flourish and Macbeth and Lady Macbeth, dressed in their royal robes, were about to drink the health of their guests when one of the murderers appeared in the shadows. He had come to tell Macbeth that Banquo was well and truly dead, with twenty stab wounds in his body, but that Fleance had escaped. So, although he himself had died, Banquo might still turn out to be the father to a line of future kings, which was Macbeth's greatest fear.

Lady Macbeth wondered who her husband was talking to in the shadows and she called to him to come to the table. The wine cups had been filled and the guests were waiting to drink his health. So Macbeth sent the murderer away and returned to drink a welcome to his fellow thanes and their wives.

'How sad it is', he said, 'that our dear friend Banquo cannot be with us. No matter, we will remember him in his absence. Let the cups be raised and let us wish him long life and happiness!'

As they raised their cups Macbeth turned to Banquo's place at the table. A moment ago it was empty, now his ghost sat there, deathly white and streaming with blood, nodding his head as if to say 'Yes, it is I, your dear friend Banquo, and see what you have done to me!'

At this horrible sight the cup fell from Macbeth's hand and crashed on the stone floor. He screamed at the ghost to go away. For the moment it vanished and he tried to collect himself. Then it appeared again and he was almost out of his mind with fear and horror, and behaved so wildly that the feast broke up and the guests hurriedly departed, astonished at what had happened. They had seen no ghost. To them Banquo's place at the table had remained empty. It seemed to them that Macbeth had suddenly gone out of his mind.

When all the guests had gone Macbeth tried to calm himself.
But he could not take his eyes off Banquo's chair. Had it really
been a ghost sitting there or was it only his imagination? At last
to prove he was no longer afraid, he went to the chair and sat in
it, resting his hands on the two arms and gripping them firmly
with his fingers. Yes, the chair was solid and the table was solid
and the flagstones beneath his feet were solid. There had been
no ghost. His imagination had been playing tricks with him.

But suddenly he felt his fingers wet and sticky and when he
lifted them from the chair there was blood on them. So
Banquo's ghost really had been sitting there, bleeding from the
gashes in his neck and arms! When he saw this Macbeth was
overcome with horror and when he held out his bloodstained
hands to his wife she was horrified, too. In the ordinary way she
would have tried to comfort him, adding her strength to his as
she had so often done in the past. Now she was at breaking
point and could not help him. So when he told her what he
meant to do next day she did not protest.

'Tomorrow' he said, 'I will go to the witches, and force them to tell me more. I am too deep in sin ever to be forgiven, but at least I shall know what dangers I have to face in the future.' So, without knowing it, he was turning for help to the creatures who had been planning his ruin from the very beginning. Wrapping his cloak around him he rode out onto the moorland to find them.

For ordinary people their cave would have been impossible to discover, but they themselves guided him along the twisting moorland paths until he suddenly found himself at its entrance. As he plunged down the rocky steps he could already hear them chanting one of their songs as they threw into their cauldron the horrible things they had been collecting that day.

Gathering all his courage Macbeth silenced them and demanded to know their deepest secrets. Could they show him what the future held in store for him? How could he be sure that the Fates were on his side, instead of on the side of his foes?

From their cauldron the witches called up three spirits, all of whom gave Macbeth the very advice he felt he needed to comfort and reassure him.

The first spirit was in the shape of a man's head floating in the steam. In a deep voice it told Macbeth that Macduff would prove to be his deadliest enemy and that he must at all costs beware of him. Then it sank back into the cauldron.

The second spirit, a naked bloodstained child, assured him that no man born of woman could ever harm him. And why should he question the word 'born'? How could he know that behind that simple word lay the wickedest trick the witches had ever played?

The third spirit was another child, holding the branch of a tree, as if sheltering behind it, and telling Macbeth that he could never be beaten until Birnam Wood came to Dunsinane. And this only made him laugh for Birnam and Dunsinane were more than twenty miles apart and only a fool would pretend that trees could uproot themselves and move!

All this so raised his confidence that Macbeth then dared to ask the question that had been haunting him for so long. Was it true that the children of Banquo and their children, on and on down the ages, would eventually be the kings of Scotland? Had he committed such fearful crimes only for their sake?

This question was followed by strange unearthly music and a mutter of distant thunder, then a procession of eight spirits came slowly and silently from the back of the cavern, all dressed as kings and wearing royal crowns. Last of all came Banquo, still bleeding and deathly pale, but smiling and happy because he knew he had not died in vain. His sons and grandsons would one day wear the crown, just as the witches had foretold. At this sight Macbeth turned away and rushed out into the night.

Lady Macbeth

Now that he knew the worst he became desperate and resolved to carry his wickedness to the very end. He would kill everyone who stood in his way. First of all he sent the two men who had killed Banquo to kill Macduff. But Macduff had already begun to suspect that Macbeth had murdered both Duncan and Banquo and that he might be next on the list. So when the murderers arrived at his castle he was already on his way to England, to join Malcolm. In their fury the murderers killed his wife and little children instead. And that was the worst crime Macbeth ever committed, even worse than killing Duncan.

Now he was deeper in sin than ever before. But his punishment was at hand, for Malcolm had persuaded the King of England to help him, and by the time Macduff arrived the King had already called his army together for the long march to Scotland, to face Macbeth in battle and to turn him off the throne and kill him.

Just as they were about to start, the Thane of Ross arrived and told Macduff what had happened to his wife and children. At first Macduff was stunned and almost collapsed. Then his grief turned to a terrible anger. He was already determined to bring Macbeth to battle. Now his determination was strengthened a hundredfold.

But before that could happen Macbeth had another crisis to suffer. When his wife went back to Duncan's bedroom to lay the daggers beside the two guards and saw the old King lying in a pool of blood, he reminded her of her father whom she had deeply loved, and this memory had stayed at the back of her mind ever since. Now the witches knew that if only they could destroy Lady Macbeth it would go a long way towards destroying her husband as well. So they made a model of her brain and removed the part that controlled the memory. At first it was cold and dead, but they sang to it and warmed it gently over the fire so that her own memory began to stir and spring to life and she began to recall the night of Duncan's murder in all its horror.

Soon she began to walk in her sleep, rubbing her hands together as if trying to wash the blood away.

'Out, out, damned spot!' she muttered. And then, in an agony of remorse: 'Will these hands never be clean?' But she knew, even in her sleep, that the stain was not on her hands at all, but on her soul, and that it would stay there forever. She grew weaker every day and began to lose her reason. Up till now she had added her resolution to her husband's, but now she could no longer help him. Now he was quite alone.

Still he kept up his courage. The witches had assured him that he would never be beaten until Birnam Wood came striding over the hills to Dunsinane, and even if by some miracle that should happen, no man born of woman could ever harm him. So why should he fear? He would win the coming battle, then he and his wife could put the past behind them and forget the wicked things they had done to gain the throne. So he gathered his army and retired to his castle at Dunsinane, the strongest castle in all Scotland. Here he would be safe. No-one could ever break down these walls. He placed watchmen on the highest towers, then put on his armour and waited for the enemy to attack.

Suddenly there came a cry from one of the watchmen. Looking towards Birnam he had seen what looked like a woodland advancing towards the castle. Unbeknown to Macbeth, the English army had cut branches from the forest trees and holding them so that the gleam of their armour would not be seen, were now advancing towards Dunsinane. When the spirit told him that he could never be killed until Birnam Wood came to Dunsinane, Macbeth had laughed. Now he understood what it meant and he began to wonder if perhaps the second part of the prophecy, the part which assured him that no man born of woman could ever kill him, might not also be a trick.

But he brushed away his fears. All the witches' promises had come true. Why should he lose faith in them because one piece of their prophecy had a double meaning? If he had been clever enough he might have understood that the moving forest would consist of branches held in front of an advancing army, not a forest actually moving. No, the witches had told him the truth and he was a fool not to have understood.

Suddenly there came a cry from within the castle and the doctor came out on to the battlements to tell him that his wife had died. Sleepless nights filled with the memory of Duncan's murder had proved too much for her, and she had given up the struggle. Macbeth had no time to grieve for her and arrange a solemn burial, for the English soldiers had now thrown away the branches and were already thundering at the castle gates. Malcolm had come to avenge his murdered father, Macduff his wife and innocent children.

All day long the battle raged and Macbeth was borne up by the witches' promise that no man born of woman could ever harm him. And when at last he came face to face with Macduff it was the witches' promise which kept up his spirit and encouraged him to taunt Macduff, telling him he was wasting his time to fight someone so magically protected by the Fates. Only then did Macduff spring the trap which the witches had long ago prepared, and which they had kept hidden behind their wicked encouragements.

'My mother's birth pains went on so long' he said, 'that they almost killed her. So a surgeon was sent for and he took me from her womb as many babies have been taken from their mothers. I can truly claim that I was never born.'

So that was the meaning of the bloodstained child rising in the steam! The blood was not its own but its mother's! Now at last Macbeth knew the worst. The witches had been trifling with him. All the hopes and promises they had held out to him had been hollow and he cursed them for their trickery and double-dealing.

At first he refused to fight, knowing in his heart that Macduff would kill him. But he must either fight or give in and be taken prisoner, and to a man as brave and proud as Macbeth that would be worse than being killed. So he resolved to fight it out.

'Before my body' he shouted, 'I throw my warlike shield!
Lay on Macduff; and damned be he who first cries
Hold, Enough!'

And gathering up the last shreds of his courage, he hurled himself at Macduff like a wild beast. If he was doomed to die, Macduff should die as well. With a dreadful clash of swords, they met. But Macduff was too strong for him. Besides, he remembered what Macbeth had done to his wife and children and that increased his fury. So at last Macbeth fell, pierced by many wounds and Macduff hacked off his head and held it up for the men on both sides to see.

'Behold the usurper's cursed head' he cried, 'the time is free!'

So the battle ended. Macbeth's soldiers threw down their weapons and the castle gates were opened and the English army streamed in with Malcolm at its head. And the soldiers went back to their homes and for a while peace returned to Scotland.

But peace has to be watched and guarded. Its enemies are always ready to break it, for the forces of evil never sleep. All day long the witches had been watching the battle, keeping up Macbeth's confidence to the very end, encouraging him to believe that he could never be killed. But when it was all over they came out from behind the rocks to find the place where he had died. There, among the gorse and rough grass lay the blood that poured out when Macduff cut off his head, and amongst the blood some pieces of skin from his neck and some hair from his beard. They screamed with joy as they gathered up these horrible fragments and carried them back to their cave. They threw them into the cauldron and blew up the fire and started dancing round it once again, singing their terrible song:

'Fair is foul and foul is fair
Hover through the fog and filthy air!'

A Midsummer Night's Dream

Cobweb

Puck

Mustardseat

Chickweed

Puck

ONG, long ago, in a tiny village in the heart of Warwickshire, there lived two good friends, Peter Quince a carpenter, and Nicholas Bottom a weaver. Peter was the finest carpenter in the whole county, and his work was known for miles and miles around, especially in making houses which at that time were mostly constructed of oak frameworks very cunningly put together, then filled in with a sort of plaster, or with brickwork made up into beautiful patterns.

Now oak-wood is very hard to work so your tools have to be kept razor sharp, and some of the joints used in making these houses were very hard to do. But Peter could do them all, and make them fit so tight you would think that the pieces of wood had lived together ever since they were born. He could do you face-lipped squint-butted scarfs with secret bridles and edge pegs, or stop-splayed scarfs with under-squinted square butts, or lap dovetails with over-squinted shoulders, or bare-faced soffit-tenons with mortise and peg, and if you had asked him he could have done box-tenons on returned timber through bridled mitres, but he didn't like those so much.

Bottom was just as good at weaving as Peter was at carpentry. At that time all cloth was woven at home, often in quite tiny cottages, not in big factories like it is today, and the village weaver was just as important as the village carpenter. So Peter and Bottom were two of the chief men in the village and everyone looked up to them. Bottom was tall and strong and had red hair and a big flat nose and a very loud voice, but his hands were like a lady's, with fine gentle fingers and it would have done you good to see him handling the yarn and threading the bobbins and folding the cloth as it came off his loom. He could weave pretty well any sort of cloth you asked him for, kersey or lindsey-wolsey or taffeta or buckram or damask or flannel or serge or velour or callamancoe or mocadoe or busy-yarn. That'll show you how good he was!

Now Peter had been a very good reader at school, so good in fact that if he went to do carpentry at some big house in the neighbourhood, he would ask if he could go into the library during his dinner hour and take down some of the fine books from their shelves and sit reading them while he ate his bread and cheese. You must remember that in the old days books were very scarce and expensive, so amongst the ordinary people you might find only half a dozen in a whole village, and they would nearly all be bibles and prayer books and little books of grammar and arithmetic. But Peter wanted adventure stories, especially stories of the ancient heroes who had lived thousands of years ago.

Well, he was so polite and he was such a good carpenter and his hands were always so clean that the gentlemen who owned these big houses would generally say 'Yes, of course you can go into the library'. And there he would sit for a whole hour reading about the voyages of the great seamen and the lives of the noble Romans and legends of the great gods and heroes who had done such wonderful things in days of old, much more wonderful things than ever happened in Warwickshire, transforming themselves into animals and fighting with terrible monsters and carrying mountains on their shoulders and having love affairs with each other's wives. Peter didn't want a love affair with anybody else's wife, he loved his own wife too much. Still, he was very interested to read the things these ancient heroes and gods and goddesses had got up to in their spare time, so interested in fact that he often forgot to eat his bread and cheese! And, of course, when he got home he would tell these stories to his friend Bottom, and Bottom liked them as much as Peter did.

Naturally, various other people in the village got to hear that Peter had read all these wonderful stories and that he was telling them to his friend Bottom as they sat among the planes and chisels and sawdust of Peter's workshop at the end of the day, and they asked him if they could come and listen as well.

First came Snug. He was a joiner, which was also a kind of carpenter, but one who did more delicate work than Peter was used to doing. Snug could make tables and chairs and beautiful stools and spiral staircases and the fine panelling which covered the walls of most rich people's houses. It was cut with special planes and made to look like folded cloth, although it was really made of oak, the very hard wood that I told you about.

He tapped at the workshop door one evening and Peter asked him in and sat him down on the sawing horse beside the bench, and when Peter's wife Betsy brought out a jug of ale, Peter told her to go back and get another mug, so that Snug could join them in a drink. And in the end Betsy had to bring no less than six mugs and a specially large jug of ale, because three other people heard all about Peter's storytelling and asked if they could come and listen as well.

The first was Flute the bellows-mender. In this long-time-ago that I am telling you about, people used to keep their log fires smouldering all through the night, then blow them up in the morning with the bellows, which usually hung on a nail beside the fireplace.

The next one who asked if he could come and hear the stories was Snout, the tinker. He made pots and pans and fine kettles out of copper and thin sheets of iron which he could bend into all sorts of wonderful shapes with his tools. His kettles were famous for miles around. If you had one of Snout's kettles you were really somebody! People would say 'Ah, I see you've got a Snout kettle' and you could say 'Yes, he made it for me specially'. They came in all sizes from one pint to ten and the finely made lids dropped into place like birds dropping into their nests.

Last came Starveling the tailor. He was seventy-two years old and had only one eye, and that one was colour-blind, so if he made you a pair of trousers they could easily finish up with different coloured legs, and as his wife had died many years ago and he worked all by himself, there was no-one to tell him when he made a mistake. He also had a touch of arthritis in his right hand so his cutting-out wasn't too good, and his tape measure was so old he couldn't read the figures on it. But everybody loved him and after all what does it matter if your trousers do have different coloured legs, so long as they cover you up and keep you warm!

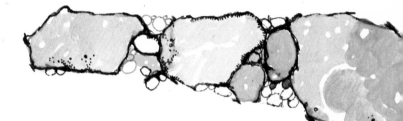

So there were these five neighbours listening in the twilight to Peter Quince telling marvellous stories of olden times in far-away Greece; of Hercules the strongest man who ever lived, of Daedalus teaching his son Icarus to fly, of Jason and the Golden Fleece and, most exciting of all, the story of Theseus killing the terrible Minotaur.

The Theseus story was one of their favourites and they made Peter tell it again and again, especially the part about the Minotaur, which had the body of a powerful man and the head and shoulders of a bull, and which lived inside a labyrinth (that's a sort of maze full of winding passages, easy to get into but almost impossible to get out of once you're in) on the island of Crete, about a hundred miles south of the Greek mainland.

Now Crete had beaten Greece in war, so as a punishment the Greeks had to send seven young men and seven young girls across the sea to Crete every year and when they arrived they were put into the labyrinth and when the Minotaur found them he crushed them to death. This had happened for many, many years and the people of Greece used to weep bitterly when the boat carrying the seven young men and seven young girls sailed away each year never to return.

But at last Theseus, the young king of Greece, made up his mind to kill this terrible monster and here's how he did it. He volunteered to go with the six other young men and the seven girls and under his cloak he hid a short sword. And when the fourteen were put into the labyrinth, Theseus led the way and met the Minotaur face to face and drew his sword and slashed at his throat and made such a deep wound that the monster fell, pouring with blood, and died. And so Greece was freed at last from the terrible curse of sending fourteen of its finest young people to be slaughtered each year. Peter also told them how, when he got back to Greece, Theseus had conquered an army of war-like maidens called Amazons and had married their beautiful queen, Hippolyta.

Theseus

The Minotaur

Pyramus

But there was one story they loved even more than the adventures of Theseus and that was the one about Pyramus and Thisbe. It was not, of course, so heroic. There was no monster and no battle and no hero king returning in triumph to marry a warrior maiden, but only a simple love story such as happened every day in the village, even though most of the love stories in the village ended happily and this one didn't.

Pyramus and Thisbe lived next door to one another in the Athens of long ago, and they wanted to become engaged and get married. But their parents didn't get on with each other and forbade them to meet. So they found a little crack in the wall that separated their two bedrooms, a tiny chink where the woodwork had shrunk and the plaster dried a little too quickly. And through this they used to whisper to each other when their parents and the others had gone to bed, saying how much they loved each other and how much they longed to touch hands and lips and be together as man and wife. And they would exchange whispered kisses and endearments and press their fingers into the crack so that their fingertips met and they felt the thrill that we all feel when we touch the hand of a much-loved friend or playmate. They felt they belonged to each other.

But at last they could bear it no longer and decided to wait for a moonlight night and run away together and get married. When they found out, their parents would have to make the best of it. So they made a plan, which they secretly whispered to each other through the crack in their bedroom walls. They would slip out of their houses at night and meet in the churchyard close to the tomb of an old man named Ninus, who had died many, many years ago. Then they would run away together to a distant city and get married without anyone knowing.

Thisbe went first, creeping quietly downstairs in case someone should hear her and carefully lifting the latch of the back door. She was wrapped up in her cloak against the cold night air and wore a white silken scarf around her head so that Pyramus should not miss her in the darkness. She stole along by the little back streets, keeping in the shadows as much as she

Thisbe

could, and soon came to the churchyard. But just as she reached the tomb of old Ninus, a hungry lion which had come out of the woods looking for food, came prowling down the pathway straight towards her. This frightened Thisbe so much that she turned and ran away, pulling the white scarf from her head and throwing it down onto the pathway to distract the lion's attention until she could get safely away and hide in the little grave-digger's hut outside the churchyard gate.

The lion gave a terrible roar, but stopped when he saw the scarf floating down on the pathway. He sniffed and pawed it a little, then took it in his mouth and tore it almost to pieces, leaving it lying ragged and dirty on the ground, before he followed Thisbe towards the gate of the churchyard. But when he reached the gate, Thisbe was safe inside the hut and had locked the door, so the lion slunk away to find his supper somewhere else.

A little while afterwards Pyramus arrived, and oh what a terrible shock he had when he came near the tomb! There on the ground lay Thisbe's silken scarf, all torn and dirty, and Thisbe herself nowhere to be seen. Poor Pyramus had heard the lion roar and now he felt sure that his dear Thisbe had been killed and eaten and that it was all his fault for having encouraged her to meet him like this at dead of night.

He took up the tattered remains of the scarf and pressed them to his lips and the tears poured down his cheeks as he thought of the cruel death she must have died. And it seemed to him that the only way he could possibly make amends was by dying himself. So he drew his sword and with a wild cry 'Thisbe, my love, I come to join you', he plunged it into his heart and fell bleeding to death beside the tomb.

'When she felt sure that the lion had gone away, Thisbe slipped out of the hut and ran along the path, her heart beating faster and faster at the thought of meeting Pyramus and being clasped in his arms. But when she reached the tomb, there lay Pyramus in a pool of blood, still clutching the tattered shreds of her scarf, the sword with which he had stabbed himself lying at his side.

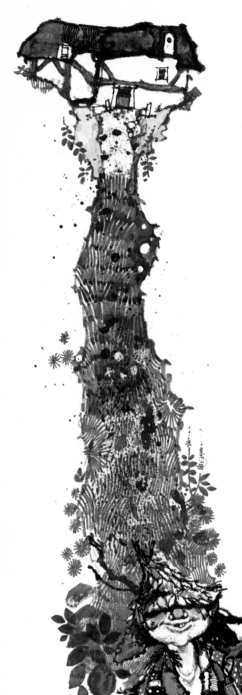

Gradually it dawned on Thisbe what had happened. Finding her torn scarf lying beside the tomb Pyramus must have thought she had been eaten alive by the lion and in despair had stabbed himself. Now, in her turn, she felt that life was not worth living, and taking up the sword with which Pyramus had killed himself, she plunged it into her own heart and fell dying over his still warm body, pressing her lips to his and murmuring his name with her dying breath.

Of all the stories Peter told in the silence of his workshop with the moonlight shining through the open window that was their favourite. That was the one they understood best. The gods and goddesses and heroes were all very fine, but Pyramus and Thisbe reminded them of the days when they were young themselves and of the torments of love they had all suffered, and they made Peter tell it over and over again.

But sometimes Starveling would tell them a story of Robin Goodfellow, the mischievous little elf who lived in the woods only a few miles away, of how he would come tip-toeing into the village at dead of night and steal a pint of milk or half a pound of salt from the larder, and how people would come downstairs in the morning and find the whole house swept and dusted and the pots and pans cleaned and the brass candlesticks on the mantlepiece all shining like gold because Robin never took anything away without doing some work in return. It was said that he and the rest of the English fairies were really descendants of people who had hidden in the woods when the Romans and Saxons and other conquerors came to Britain hundreds of years before and that they had gradually grown smaller and smaller because there was no salt in the woods and it is salt which helps you to grow. So they had to come out at night and steal some from the cottages near the woods.

Although this little elf's full name was Robin Goodfellow, he was usually called Puck. He was mischievous but very kind and if he visited your home at night it was said that you would be lucky for a whole year, and some people would leave a basin-full of milk outside the back door, with a box of salt beside it, in the hope that he would choose their house for his next visit. He was one foot four and three-quarter inches high and wore a tiny pointed cap made of beech leaves, stuck together on a framework of little cedar twigs, and his clothes were made of patchwork pieces which he had taken from people's cupboards at night, pieces of worn-out cloaks or ladies stockings and petticoats all neatly stitched together with strong grass.

Or Flute would tell the story of Oberon and Titania, the king and queen of the fairies, who had come over to England long before the Romans and had settled in the Warwickshire woods, because they were tired of the hot sun of India and loved the beautiful English countryside with its trees and hedgerows and wild flowers and had lived there for thousands of years. Puck was small, but Oberon and Titania were really tiny, only three and three quarter inches and two and seven eighths inches high (you measure that with your ruler and you'll see how tiny it is!), and they had taken up with some little English fairies, Peaseblossom, Cobweb, Moth and Mustardseed and the tiniest of all, little baby Chickweed, and formed a complete colony.

They had built a palace among the outspreading roots of a great beech tree and there they lived and held their Court. In winter-time they shut the doors and closed up all the holes in the roof and went to sleep, waiting for the spring and summer to come round again. Then they would come out and start dancing in their magic rings, making beautiful patterns as they criss-crossed each other in the moonlight, clapping their tiny hands and singing little songs in praise of their king and queen.

So the storytelling went on night after night, but always it came back to Theseus saving the lives of so many beautiful young boys and girls by killing the Minotaur, half man and half beast, in the labyrinth at Crete, then going home to marry Hippolyta the beautiful queen of the Amazons. And to round off the evening, the simple tale of Pyramus and Thisbe, which

45

A troupe of actors

they loved best of all. That was the one Peter always ended up with before they finished the last few drops of ale and said goodnight to each other and went home to bed.

Now in those days there were hardly any proper theatres, so actors used to travel from village to village giving performances wherever they could find a suitable place, on a common or village green or even in a churchyard. The plays they did were mostly taken from the Bible, the story of Adam and Eve and Cain and Abel and Noah's Ark and Daniel in the Lion's Den, leading up to the coming of Jesus and his disciples and their wonderful work healing and teaching beside the Sea of Galilee. So you could learn all about God in the form of plays, instead of having to listen to the preacher telling it from the pulpit. And one day a troupe of actors came to the village where Peter and Bottom and the other four lived, and did their plays on a simple platform made of planks laid on top of empty barrels; and the whole village turned out to see them.

They acted the plays very well, but Nick Bottom thought that if he and Peter and the others could get up a play of their own they could do it much better, especially if they could make a play out of one of Peter's stories. After all, they already knew the Bible story. Everybody in England knew it. But hardly anyone knew these stories from Greece, the wonderful tales of people who lived long before Jesus was born. The story would have to be a simple one because they were only beginners and wouldn't be able to learn long speeches. And it must not have a lot of characters in it because there were only six of them and they would not want to act more than one part each. But they already had the right story, their favourite, the story of Pyramus and Thisbe. That was simple enough. The only problem was making the story into a play, which is a very difficult thing to do. That would have to be Peter's job. He was the best at reading and writing, surely he could write a play as good as some of the ones they had seen!

So Peter took on the job, and worked very hard at it, and when the parts were written out and they had their first rehearsal in the workshop it sounded very fine.

46

At first Bottom wanted to choose who would act the various parts, but Peter wasn't having any of that nonsense. He had written the play and he was determined it should be performed the way he wanted it. So, for the moment at any rate, Bottom gave in with a good grace, and agreed that Peter should do the choosing.

Of course Bottom had to be Pyramus, because Pyramus was the hero and had the biggest part. It was also a very sad part which meant that Bottom could pretend to cry and that would

Peter Quince

47

Starveling

Bottom roars....

Snout

48

make the audience cry as well, and people in the audience always enjoy a good cry.

Next to be chosen was Flute the bellows-mender. Peter had put him down for Thisbe because he was young and slim and had fair curly hair. At first he objected because he had just started growing a beard, but Peter said it didn't show very much and no-one would notice it. 'Besides,' he said, 'you've got a nice high voice, and that's just what we want for Thisbe.' 'But I can do a high voice, too,' said Bottom. 'Why can't I be Thisbe as well as Pyramus?', and he suddenly went off into a little squeaky voice like a girl's. But once again Peter was firm, and insisted that Flute would be the best Thisbe, with Starveling as his mother, Snout as Pyramus's father and Peter himself as Thisbe's father.

Last came the part of the lion, and that was given to Snug. But once again there was trouble. Bottom said he must play the lion because he had the loudest voice. He could roar loud enough to lift the roof off, and he gave a sample there and then, roaring till the rafters of the workshop fairly trembled. Then he said that if that was too loud, he could just as easily roar very softly, and he gave them a sample of his soft roaring, which was more like a cat purring or a dove cooing. But once again Peter put his foot down. Bottom must play Pyramus and Pyramus only. And so it was agreed, and they all tucked their scripts into their pockets and went off home to learn their parts ready for the first rehearsal.

The next day Bottom came to see Quince. He had something very important to ask him. How should they let the village and the people living all round know the name of the play and when and where it was to be performed, and the names of the actors? And how much should they charge people to come and see it? Peter scratched his head and thought. Then he said: 'I know, we'll write it out on pieces of paper and nail them up on posts all over the village. We'll call them "posters" and you can do the nailing-up.' And he went and fetched pen and ink and paper and started writing. 'The moste lamentable comedie and moste cruel death of Pyramus and Thisbe. Taken from ye Greeke. Writte by Master Peter Quince, with ye following actors in ye leading partes.' 'That means my name must come first,' said Bottom. 'Pyramus comes first in the title and B comes before all the others in the alphabet.'

So that's how it was written down. First Bottom, then Flute, then all the rest. 'Tickets price two pence obtainable at ye doores. Proceedes in aide of ye poore and needie of this parishe. Performance to beginne at seven of ye clocke sharply.'

They all worked very hard rehearsing their parts, though it wasn't very easy keeping Bottom under control. He kept trying to make alterations in the play, especially if it made his own part stand out more. But Peter stuck to his guns and gradually it all came together just as he had written it. The biggest difficulty was to find some way of showing the crack in the wall between the two bedrooms. How on earth do you show such a thing on the stage? There was also the fact that Pyramus and Thisbe had run away by moonlight, so that had to be shown as well. In the end it was agreed that Snug should hold up his two forefingers just a quarter of an inch apart to show the crack in the wall, and that Pyramus and Thisbe should speak to each other in a loud whisper standing each side of the two fingers. And that Starveling should hold up a lantern all through the play to show that it was taking place in moonlight.

They rehearsed for a whole month every night. At six o'clock sharp Peter would finish his carpentry and square up the workshop, then Bottom would give it a good sweep, then the others would arrive and set out the stools and light the candle in the lantern, and Mrs Nick would bring out a big jug of ale and six mugs and some bread and cheese, and away they would go, working hard till nine or ten, following Peter's instructions and trying to get it as perfect as possible.

As the day of the performance came nearer, they grew more and more excited, especially Bottom. He was a big strong fellow, and you would have thought him the most cool-headed of the lot. But it was Peter who stayed the coolest and Bottom who got the most nervous, until the night before the performance he was sweating with excitement and Mrs Nick found it hard to keep him quiet. As they lay in bed together, Nick made her go through his part five times over to make sure he had got every word right. And it was twelve o'clock before he blew out the candle and fell into a troubled sleep.

All night long he tossed and turned because in his sleep he
was having a strange and wonderful dream. King Theseus had
invited them to go to Athens and give their performance at his
wedding with Hippolyta. And suddenly there they were, all
dressed in strange clothes and shaking hands with some of the
most important people in the whole of Greece. And Theseus
said he wanted the play kept a dead secret, so he would like
them to do their final rehearsal in a little open space in a wood
outside the city.

Bottom turned restlessly in his sleep, and pulled the
bedclothes over to his side, but Mrs Nick pulled them back and
told him to lie still.

Then he dreamt that as Peter was sweeping out the wood
they found some tiny little fairies among the leaves, and when
they picked them up they said their names were Oberon and
Titania, and that they were the king and queen of all the fairies
in England and that Peter need not do any more sweeping
because they had five very efficient little servants, Peaseblossom, Cobweb, Moth and Mustardseed and little baby
Chickweed, and they would do all the sweeping that was
necessary.

Now that very morning Titania had been quarrelling with
Oberon and had been very rude to him and Oberon was
determined to get his own back on her, but for the moment he
pretended that everything was normal and he said how much he
and Titania were looking forward to seeing the rehearsal and
that they hoped Peter and Bottom and the others would come
dancing with them when it was over.

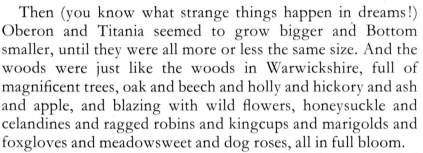

Helena

Demetrius

Then (you know what strange things happen in dreams!) Oberon and Titania seemed to grow bigger and Bottom smaller, until they were all more or less the same size. And the woods were just like the woods in Warwickshire, full of magnificent trees, oak and beech and holly and hickory and ash and apple, and blazing with wild flowers, honeysuckle and celandines and ragged robins and kingcups and marigolds and foxgloves and meadowsweet and dog roses, all in full bloom.

And Titania turned a foxglove flower right-side up, and filled it with ale, and the actors were given harebells for mugs and suddenly they were all drinking a health to Peaseblossom, Cobweb, Moth and Mustardseed and little baby Chickweed, and saying thank you to them for sweeping up so nicely.

Then the rehearsal started, but it had no sooner begun than it all seemed to disappear and they were back in the palace with Theseus, and an old man named Egeus was complaining that his daughter Hermia was refusing to marry Demetrius, the young man he had chosen for her. She wanted to marry a young fellow named Lysander instead; and Egeus begged Theseus to tell her that she must do as she was told.

But Hermia said how could she? Her friend Helena was in love with Demetrius, and he had often said he loved her as well, so now he really ought to marry her. But King Theseus said Hermia must obey her father and marry Demetrius. If she didn't she would be severely punished.

So Hermia and Lysander agreed that the only thing to do was to run away and get married somewhere outside the city, then come back and confess to Theseus what they had done. That night they slipped out of their two houses, just like Pyramus and Thisbe in the story, but in the dark they lost their way and landed up in the middle of the wood where Bottom and Peter and Snout and Flute and Snug and Starveling were rehearsing their play.

Soon afterwards Demetrius came running into the wood
hoping to steal Hermia away from Lysander before he had time
to marry her, then came Helena running after Demetrius whom
she still loved so dearly.

When Oberon saw how unkind Demetrius was being to
Helena, telling her to go back home and to stop being so silly,
he felt sorry for her and he called for Puck, the very same
mischievous little Puck that Starveling had told them all about
in Peter's workshop. For some strange reason he had now
become Oberon's chief helper and a sort of messenger boy, I
suppose because he could take himself on long journeys very,
very quickly, to places like Africa and China and India and be
back again before you could say winking. Peaseblossom,
Cobweb, Moth and Mustardseed and little baby Chickweed
were kind and beautiful and they were very fine dancers and had
exquisite manners and they looked after Titania like perfect
little maids of honour, but they had only very tiny brains so you
couldn't ask them to do anything very difficult. Also their
wings were so small they couldn't fly very far or very fast, so it
had to be Puck for the very special job that Oberon had in
mind.

Oberon told him to nip round to the other side of the world
and bring back a spray of a wonderful herb called Love-in-
Idleness. This herb had a blue flower with a yellow bulb
hanging beside it and the bulb contained a magic juice and if
you took this magic juice and squeezed a tiny drop into people's
eyes while they were asleep, they would fall deeply in love with
the first person they saw when they awoke. And not only with a
person. It could just as easily be with an animal, a giraffe or a
polar bear or a hamster. Oberon meant to squeeze some of this
magic juice into Titania's eyes and arrange for her to fall in love
with something really ugly as soon as she woke up. That would
pay her out for having been so rude to him in the morning.

He would also get Puck to squeeze some of the juice into Demetrius's eyes as soon as he grew tired and fell asleep. Then he would arrange that the first person Demetrius would see when he woke up would be Helena and that meant he would be in love with her all over again as he had been only a little while ago and as Hermia and Lysander were in love with each other now. Then all would end happily.

When Bottom heard that everything was going to end happily he rolled over in bed and gave Mrs Nick a hug, then went off to sleep and drifted away into dreamland again.

Once more it was moonlight and they were still in the woodland outside Athens rehearsing the play and Puck had just returned from his trip round the world, bringing back the spray of Love-in-Idleness, also leaves from two other magic herbs, Sweet Normality and another one that only he knew about, called Shaggy Hee-Haw.

He knew that Oberon loved Titania too much to want to go on punishing her for very long, so whatever stupid or ugly creature she fell in love with when she woke up, he would soon want to bring her back to normal and for that he would need two little leaves of Sweet Normality to lay on her eyelids.

The Shaggy Hee-Haw Puck meant to use in quite another way. He had watched Bottom rehearsing, pretending to be a great lover and whispering to Thisbe and then stabbing himself with a wooden sword and making a silly speech before he died, and it was so bad it had made him laugh. He thought that if an actor could pretend as badly as Bottom was pretending, it was time somebody gave him something to really pretend about and that's where the Shaggy Hee-Haw would come in.

But first Oberon had to squeeze the magic Love-in-Idleness into Titania's eyes, and this he did, stealing softly into her scented bower just as she was nodding off and laughing quietly to himself as he crept out again, brushing aside the honeysuckle as he passed.

Next Puck had to find Demetrius and squeeze some Love-in-Idleness into his eyes, so that when he woke he would fall back into love with Helena. And this is where he made the first mistake he had ever made in his life! He was so busy thinking of the trick he was going to play on Bottom with the Shaggy Hee-Haw that he dropped the Love-in-Idleness into Lysander's eyes instead of into Demetrius's, which meant that if Helena was the first person Lysander saw when he woke up he would be in love with her instead of with his dear Hermia and that would be terrible wouldn't it?

Oberon saw at once what a silly mistake Puck had made and told him to go and put it right. So Puck ran at once to find Demetrius and put some Love-in-Idleness into his eyes as he had been told to do at first. But then he made another mistake,

Lysander

Helena

Demetrius

the kind of mistake that's always happening in dreams. He forgot to lay some Sweet Normality on Lysander's eyes. So you can guess what happened now!

Lysander and Demetrius both woke up just as Helena came running past trying to find Demetrius and they both saw her at the same moment, and both fell head-long in love with her, Demetrius who had spent half the night trying to escape from her, and Lysander who was supposed to be head over ears in love with Hermia and only running away with her in order to marry her.

I am not sure whether Puck really made a mistake or whether he did it on purpose. But you can imagine how Hermia felt when she woke up and saw Demetrius madly in love with Helena again and and Lysander chasing after her as well. It was one of the biggest muddles you can possibly imagine. Certainly Puck enjoyed seeing both Lysander and Demetrius running after Helena, and Helena looking astonished to find both young men trying to make love to her at the same time.

But then Puck did something else and this certainly was no mistake, it was done on purpose. He took a large leaf of Shaggy Hee-Haw out of his little pouch and dropped a piece of it into a foxglove flower full of ale which Titania had left behind a bush near to where the actors were rehearsing, so that they could refresh themselves when they felt tired.

55

Now acting, especially acting a difficult part like Pyramus, makes you very thirsty, so that when Bottom had finished his first scene with Flute, whispering to him through the crack in the wall, he went behind the bush to have a little drink, and there was the foxglove flower full of lovely ale with a nice creamy head on its top. So he lifted it to his lips and took a long, long swig. Your father will tell you what a swig is. It's something between a gulp and a guzzle, and it feels lovely as it goes down.

Now what I haven't told you is that when you drink a foxglove flower full of ale that has a piece of Shaggy Hee-Haw leaf in it, your head suddenly starts to change into a donkey's! And that's what happened to Bottom. First his ears started to grow long, then his nose, then he began to make funny noises, as he blew the froth off the top of the ale. And suddenly there he was, a decent law-abiding Warwickshire weaver, with his actor's script sticking out of his pocket, and a donkey's head growing out of his shoulders. And for the first few minutes all he could say was 'Hee-haw, hee-haw, hee-haw', pure donkey talk, instead of proper English words! And Puck was watching all this from his hiding-place behind a hawthorn bush and laughing his little head off.

But his mischief was not finished yet. He knew why Oberon had put the Love-in-Idleness into Titania's eyes and now he thought he would tie his little piece of mischief up into a perfect knot. So he climbed into Titania's bower and pinched her hand. And, of course, that woke her up. And as she sat up blinking and rubbing her eyes, who should she see but Bottom with a donkey's head on his shoulders sitting on a tree stump watching the rehearsal.

And just as Oberon had planned, Titania fell headlong in love with him. Just imagine Titania, the most beautiful fairy in all the world, falling in love with a donkey! But that's exactly what happened. In fact, she was so much in love with him that she invited him into her bower and kissed his soft wet nose and stroked his ears. And she cuddled him and fondled him and made such a fuss of him that he hardly knew whether he was on his head or his heels. And she tangled moss roses in his hair and sent her little servants out to get him a specially nice feed of oats and hay.

Now Oberon had been so interested watching the rehearsal—Snug had just found Thisbe's scarf and was tearing it to pieces, roaring away like mad—that he hadn't noticed what Puck had been up to. When he did see, he gave him a good shaking and told him to go and put everything back to normal.

So now Puck took the sprig of Sweet Normality out of his pocket and rushed round persuading people to sit still while he laid some little pieces of it on their eyelids.

56

Lysander

And Bottom suddenly turned into a simple Warwickshire weaver again, with his original head and his old flat nose, and Titania forgot all about the silly donkey she had been so much in love with and apologised to Oberon for having been so rude to him and Lysander came back to Hermia and took her in his arms and gave her a great big kiss, all through this wonderful Sweet Normality.

The only one Puck did not give it to was Demetrius because he didn't want him to change. That was the whole idea. He had to stay in love with Helena. And Helena certainly didn't need it because she had been in love with Demetrius all the time.

So now the two pairs of lovers, Lysander and Hermia and Demetrius and Helena, went back to the palace and told King Theseus that they had sorted everything out and asked if they could get married. And King Theseus said: 'Yes, we will have a combined wedding, all six of us. I will marry Hippolyta, and you, Lysander, will marry Hermia and you, Demetrius, will marry Helena, all on the same day. And when the wedding is over we will have a wonderful feast, and after the feast I have a big surprise for you. We are going to see a play taken from one of our old Greek legends. It is being rehearsed even now out in the woods by some gentlemen from Warwickshire. I have a copy of the playbill here. And he read it out. 'The moste lamentable comedie and moste cruel death of Pyramus and Thisbe, writte by Master Peter Quince with ye following actors in ye leading partes.' And so on to the end, laughing as he read. 'Proceedes in aide of ye poore and needie of this parishe.' That means the whole of Athens! 'Performance to beginne at seven of ye clocke sharply.'

'Go,' he said to Lysander, 'get some copies made. We'll have them nailed up on posts all over the city. We'll call them "posters" and you can do the nailing-up.' And there in Bottom's dream was Lysander with hammer and nails fastening one of the playbills to the doors of the palace. Knock! knock! knock!

Of course, it was not really Lysander at all but Peter Quince knocking at the front door. He'd come to tell Nick it was time to wake up and start getting things ready for the play. And suddenly Nick scratched his head and sat up in bed and slowly began to realise that the proper performance, the one they had been working so hard at for over a month, the one at which he was going to make his reputation, had not yet happened. His visit to Athens and to the palace of King Theseus and the strange thing that had happened to his head when he drank the foxglove flower full of ale on the bank beside the hawthorn bush and the lovely time he had spent with Titania in her bower, had been all a dream. And he jumped out of bed and started getting his trousers on.

The show went wonderfully well. Bottom remembered every word of his part and did his dying speech the best he had ever done it, with real tears running down his cheeks. And Flute spoke his speeches higher up than he'd ever managed to speak before. And Snug mixed loud roaring with soft roaring so well and tore Thisbe's scarf so fiercely that even Bottom had to admit he was the best lion they could have chosen. The only thing was that Starveling's lantern kept going out and they had to wait till it could be lighted again before they could go on with the play.

The audience received the performance with loud applause, especially for Peter who had written the play and also directed and stage-managed it. And it was agreed that he must write another one and that Bottom and the others must be asked to do a performance every year.

But to this day no-one has ever discovered how Bottom came to wake up from his dream with a bunch of buttercups in his hand and his hair full of moss roses, or how Mrs Nick came to find a tiny sprig of chickweed among the bedclothes. And I don't suppose they ever will. But you and I know don't we? Nick Bottom really had been on a trip to fairyland and he was lucky to get back so easily and lucky to find his own head on his shoulders again.

59

Old Capulet

Romeo and Juliet

THIS is the story of a bitter quarrel between two rich and powerful families and of how it brought grief and bloodshed to both.

It happened more than five hundred years ago in Verona, a tiny city in the north of Italy. The two families were called Montague and Capulet and the quarrel was so old that no-one could remember how it had begun. A member of one family had perhaps said something insulting to a member of the other family. Or perhaps it had sprung from a tiny piece of gossip by someone who was not related to either family. Then it had gradually grown and each side had added to it, so that it kept blazing up at public meetings or in the street or even in church. And as all the young men in those days wore swords and daggers and kept them very sharp and were taught to use them from an early age you can see how dangerous it was to be walking in the streets of Verona when a gang of Capulets happened to run into a gang of Montagues. The Prince of Verona had often tried to make peace between the two families, but it was useless, they still went on quarrelling and fighting.

Now the Montague family had a son named Romeo, seventeen years old, dark and handsome and gentle. He did not hate the Capulets. He knew that all the quarrelling and fighting was senseless. Besides, he was deeply in love with a beautiful girl named Rosaline, and was determined to win her favour and persuade her to marry him and settle down to a peaceful life. But he happened to be a fine sword fighter, so whenever a dispute broke out between a gang of Montagues and a gang of Capulets he was sure to get dragged into it.

At last the Prince became so angry at all this stupid quarrelling that he called his advisers together and made a new law saying that anyone caught fighting in the streets would be put to death. So for a little while things quietened down. The gangs stayed indoors and there was peace in the city.

Now Romeo had two good friends, Benvolio who was, like him, a Montague, and Mercutio who belonged to neither of the quarrelling families. Benvolio was solid and stable, loyal and brave, the sort of friend you would like to have beside you in time of trouble. Mercutio was quite different. He also was loyal and brave but he had a lightning wit and a delicious sense of humour and he was always making fun of people. He and Benvolio used to tease Romeo about his love for Rosaline. 'Why,' they asked, 'should you bother with Rosaline when there are dozens of girls in Verona just as beautiful as she is, and all of them ready to fall into your arms?' And indeed they were right. But Romeo could think of no-one but Rosaline.

Rosaline was certainly beautiful, but there was at least one girl in Verona who was far more beautiful. Indeed she was one of the most beautiful girls in the whole world. She had long red-

Romeo

Benvolio

Mercutio

Old Montague

gold hair and grey-green eyes and a beautiful slim body and when she smiled it was as if the sky had opened and all the sunshine had been let out. Her name was Juliet and she was the only daughter of the Capulet family. She was still very young, only just turned fourteen, but she looked older and she was so grown up in her thoughts and ways that it would never have crossed your mind to ask how old she was. Her parents had kept her mostly at home with an old nurse who had been her nanny when she was a tiny baby and had stayed with her as a sort of companion.

So when Paris, a young relative of the Prince, asked her father if he might marry her, old Capulet was at first uncertain what to answer. Juliet was really far too young to be a wife, yet a marriage to someone so closely related to the Prince would make the Capulet family one of the most important in Verona and that was a chance not to be missed. So in the end old Capulet told Juliet to look kindly on Paris and try to love him.

In those days young girls were expected to do exactly what their parents told them to do, so Juliet obeyed. Paris was young and rich and handsome, and although Juliet didn't know him very well she knew that her father would give her a wonderful wedding and that everybody would be talking about her and saying how lucky she was to be marrying one of the most important young men in Verona.

Old Capulet and his wife were so happy when Juliet agreed to their plan that they decided to give a party for all their friends and relatives. And, of course, Paris must be there as well, so that Juliet could dance with him and get to know him better. And there would be merrymaking into the small hours of the morning, and all the men would wear masks and fancy dress so that it would be difficult to tell who they were and the girls would have great fun guessing who they had been dancing with.

When Mercutio heard about the party he dared Romeo and Benvolio to get past the door-keepers in disguise and mix with the Capulets as if they had been properly invited. Then Romeo would see for himself that Rosaline was not the only beautiful girl in Verona, and that would be very good for him. It would of course, be dangerous, for if a Montague were discovered amongst the Capulets, swords would be drawn, especially by Juliet's cousin Tybalt, who had a fiery temper and was quite fearless. He above all the rest would be enraged if he discovered that two Montagues had managed to get into the party. But surely the risk was worth taking. Rosaline would be there and Romeo could dance with her and perhaps lead her into a quiet corner of the moonlit garden, where he could talk to her and tell her how much he loved her.

So, thinking nothing of the danger, Romeo agreed. He dressed himself as a traveller who had just returned from the Holy Land and the places where Jesus had lived and worked his miracles, Nazareth and Jerusalem and the Sea of Galilee and the Mount of Olives and Calvary where he had been crucified. These travellers were called palmers and it was thought that if you could get one of them to touch you and give you his blessing some of the holiness of the places he had visited would pass from him to you. Dressed as a palmer and wearing a mask, Romeo could spend the whole evening unrecognised.

When he was disguised you would never have known him.

He found an old robe, patched and torn, and a pair of sandals so worn that you would think he had only just returned from a long, long journey, walking all the way. Only his eyes behind the mask and his beautiful soft voice gave him away. Those he could never hide.

Mercutio dressed himself as an Indian prince, in flowing robes and a brilliant-coloured turban, Benvolio as a soldier just returned from the battlefield. They knew all too well the risk they were taking, but they were young and adventurous and if they succeeded it would be something to talk about for many weeks to come. So they thought nothing of the danger, and their disguises were so good that they got into the party without any difficulty and began to mingle with the other guests as if they really had a right to be there.

As soon as they had greeted their host and hostess, Mercutio and Benvolio went into the dining-room to taste the food and wine, but Romeo was not hungry. The musicians were already entering the gallery and tuning their instruments. He wanted to find Rosaline and be the first to lead her into the dance. But suddenly he saw a beautiful young girl coming down the stairs at the opposite end of the hall and in a flash all thought of Rosaline went out of his head. For here was Juliet at her loveliest, dressed in shimmering silver shot with green. Her dress was caught up under her breast and her hair poured down her back in a golden cascade. She had been sleeping so as to be fresh for the party. Her face was flushed and her eyes shining with youth and gaiety.

Like a man in a dream Romeo walked towards her and as she reached the bottom of the stairs he took her hand and without a word led her into the centre of the floor where they began to dance. Soon others were dancing too, and Romeo and Juliet were lost in the throng of moving figures. Holding each other close they felt the thrill that no-one can explain, the thrill of knowing that they belonged to each other and must go on belonging to each other until the day they died.

Only when Juliet's mother called her away to dance with Paris was Romeo able to ask who was the lovely girl he had been dancing with, and only then did he learn that she was the daughter of old Capulet, his family's greatest foe.

Juliet also had no idea who she had been dancing with. The touch of Romeo's hands and the closeness of his body as they danced and the beautiful dark eyes gazing at her from behind the mask and the sound of his voice whispering words of love as they danced together, had quite bewitched her. But who was he? What was his name? How would she ever manage to meet him again?

Suddenly it came to her. The one person who might help was her old nurse who was serving the guests with wine. So Juliet

Romeo

Feeling along the wall, he found a stone jutting out from the rest. Using this as a foothold he vaulted onto the top of the wall, then dropped down into the orchard on the other side. Moving stealthily from tree to tree he soon found himself underneath the windows. There he waited, breathless.

At last the windows opened and Juliet stepped out on to the balcony. She whispered his name into the shadows and Romeo, from beneath the balcony, replied. Then, very quietly, they confessed how much they loved each other and how much they longed to be together and how much they wished their two families could end their hatred. Then they agreed that if only they could marry and have children the enmity might die out, then their meeting at the dance would have proved lucky. The fighting and quarrelling would stop. No more young men would be killed in the streets and everyone would bless them.

So Romeo promised to go the very next day to an old priest he had known and loved since he was a little boy and arrange for him to marry them, and early in the morning Juliet must send a messenger to find out what time he had arranged so that she could join him at the little chapel where the priest belonged and there he would be waiting for them. So Juliet promised to send her nurse at nine o'clock next morning.

Then she leaned over the balcony and stretched down her hand and Romeo stretched upwards as high as he could so that their fingers touched and once again they had the thrilling feeling that they belonged to one another and they crossed their hearts and swore to be faithful until they died. Then the nurse called that it was time Juliet was in bed, so they parted and Juliet slipped indoors and gently shut the window and Romeo climbed the wall again into the street and with Juliet's voice still filling his ears went home to bed.

But he could not sleep, and early next morning he went to the old priest telling him he wanted to marry Juliet that very day. At first the priest tried to persuade him that Juliet was too young to marry, but when he saw that Romeo was in earnest he agreed to marry them at once.

Soon the nurse arrived, sent by Juliet to find out when Romeo expected her to join him. The old woman knew that she ought to have persuaded Juliet not to be so impetuous, but she herself had married when she was little more than a girl and her marriage had been a very happy one. Besides, Juliet pleaded so hard that she had not the heart to resist. So when Romeo told her that the priest had agreed to perform the marriage ceremony that very morning, she ran back in great excitement, proud to have been let into the secret.

As soon as Juliet received Romeo's message she wrapped herself in a cloak and made her way to the chapel. There she fell into Romeo's arms and their lips met in a long, long kiss and they were saying 'I love you, I love you, I love you' again and again and again until the old priest reminded them why they had come to see him. Then they both laughed and Juliet hugged the priest and kissed him as well and he led them both to the tiny altar.

Romeo had had no time to buy a wedding ring, so while she was asleep he had crept into his mother's bedroom and taken from her jewel box a tiny silver one. It was not very precious and she would never miss it, but it made him very happy to think that the daughter of a Capulet was being married with a Montague's ring. That would be the first step in binding the two quarrelling families together.

When the wedding was over, the priest handed them a little ebony crucifix with the body of Jesus carved in ivory and they both kissed it, then knelt and prayed together on the altar steps. They had no thought for the future, no idea how or when or where they would manage to make a home together. For the moment only one thing mattered. They were now joined in marriage. They were man and wife, and no-one knew except the nurse and the old priest.

As they stood trembling with excitement beside the altar the priest reminded Juliet that her father and mother would soon be wondering what had become of her. She must hurry home if she was not to be missed. So, promising Romeo to fasten a knotted rope to her balcony so that he could come to her that night, and trusting him to settle everything for the future, she stole out of the chapel and ran swiftly home, slipping the ring into the pocket of her cloak as she ran. It might be a long time before she could wear it openly but she could always wear it round her neck, close to her heart.

Romeo went home more slowly, his heart filled with a deep happiness. In a single day he had met and married the loveliest girl in the world and that night she would lie in his arms. For the moment that was enough.

Of course, Mercutio and Benvolio could not help boasting that, along with Romeo, they had been at the Capulet's party; that no-one had recognised them and that Romeo had even danced with Capulet's daughter, holding her close and gazing

into her eyes like a lover. When he heard of this insult Juliet's cousin Tybalt took his sword and went out into the streets to find Romeo and fight with him. And it was not long before they met.

Knowing nothing of Romeo's marriage, Mercutio and Benvolio had persuaded him to join them for a glass of wine at their favourite tavern. Mercutio was in high spirits, giving wonderful imitations of old Capulet and some of the guests who had been present at the party. Indeed his imitation of Juliet's nurse was so lifelike that Romeo and Benvolio laughed until they cried. And then suddenly round the corner came Tybalt, with his sword already drawn. In flaming anger he challenged Romeo to fight, but brave as he was, Romeo refused. For Tybalt was Juliet's cousin and if Romeo should kill him how could Juliet ever forgive him?

72

Yet Tybalt's challenge could not go unanswered. If Romeo would not fight him, Mercutio would. Indeed his sword had already flashed out and in a moment he and Tybalt were locked in a fierce duel. Their swords glittered as they moved to and fro, first one gaining the advantage, then the other. At last Mercutio drove Tybalt to the wall and was about to stab him when Romeo came between them. If Mercutio were to kill Tybalt it would be almost as bad as if Romeo himself were to kill him. So, just as Mercutio was about to break through Tybalt's guard, Romeo tried to pull him away. But as he did so Tybalt passed his sword under Romeo's arm into Mercutio's body, upwards towards his heart, and Mercutio fell dying at the feet of his two friends.

For a few moments Romeo and Benvolio held Mercutio in their arms hoping against hope that he was not as badly wounded as he seemed to be, but Mercutio knew that his end was near. Still he refused to be serious and died as he had lived with a joke on his lips. For when Romeo asked him how badly he was wounded he said 'Ask for me tomorrow and you shall find me a grave man', which could have meant that instead of joking and making fun of people, he intended to be solemn and serious, but which could also mean that he would soon be dead and ready to be laid in his grave. And, of course, it was the second of the two meanings that Mercutio had in his mind. So a brave and beautiful young man met his end.

Now Romeo was sorry he had interfered in the fight. If he had kept out of it Mercutio might still be alive. Now he no longer cared that Tybalt was Juliet's cousin. His only thought was to be revenged. So when Tybalt taunted him for being a coward and letting his friend die instead of being willing to die himself, Romeo drew his sword and rushed at Tybalt in fury. The fight was short and deadly. Even when he was calm Romeo was a fine swordsman, but now he was blazing with anger. Tybalt was driven back, fighting hard, but it was useless. First his sword arm was cut, then the sword itself was struck from his hand and he drew his dagger to defend himself.

Determined to fight on equal terms, Romeo threw down his own sword and, drawing his dagger, grappled with Tybalt like a wrestler. Tybalt reeled under the attack, but Romeo was too strong for him and at last drove his dagger up to the hilt into Tybalt's heart.

Only as Tybalt fell did Romeo realise that he had done the very thing he had prevented Mercutio from doing. He had murdered the cousin of the girl who had, only a few hours before, become his wife and who would soon be waiting for him to climb up to her balcony and join his body with hers. And what was even worse, he suddenly remembered the law condemning to death anyone caught fighting in the streets of

Verona. Yet if he had not killed Tybalt, Tybalt would surely have killed him. Now he stood trembling beside the two dead bodies, wondering where he could turn for help.

In the end Benvolio agreed to go to the Prince and explain how at first Romeo had refused to fight and how Mercutio had fought in his stead, and how Mercutio's death had driven Romeo to lose his temper. Meanwhile Romeo must go to the little chapel and hide until Benvolio came to tell him what the Prince had decided.

The Prince listened patiently to Benvolio's story and after weighing the matter very carefully made a wise and merciful decision. He could not possibly break the law he had made only a few weeks before. At the same time he realised that Romeo had tried his best not to get involved in the fight, so it was not fair that he should be put to death. But without knowing it the Prince ordered a punishment almost as cruel. Romeo must leave Verona within twenty-four hours and never return. And if he did return and was caught in the city he would be immediately beheaded.

Romeo knew he must obey the Prince, but he also knew that he could never go on living without Juliet. So there was only one thing to do. They would spend their marriage night together, then in the morning he would slip away to the nearby city of Mantua which lay beyond the reach of Verona's laws. Later on Juliet could join him. Their separation would be hard to bear but it would be very brief and in the end everything would come right.

When Juliet heard about the fight she was torn between grief for Tybalt and horror that it was her husband who had killed him. But when she heard the full story her love for Romeo overcame all her doubts and she longed for the night to come, to show him that she understood how it had happened and that she knew he was not to blame.

Hidden in the little chapel, Romeo waited impatiently for the night. He longed to explain everything to Juliet as much as she longed to tell him that she understood. So as soon as it was dark, he returned to the little lane behind the Capulet's house and, finding the same outjutting stone he had used the night before, climbed the wall and made his way swiftly towards Juliet's balcony. There, fastened securely to the handrail above, hung a stout cord knotted at intervals to give foothold and handhold.

Swiftly Romeo climbed to the balcony, pulling the rope up behind him and coiling it beside the rails. Then the window opened and Juliet flew into his arms and they were both laughing and crying at the same time and running their hands through each other's hair and kissing each other wildly, knowing that this might well be the only night they would spend together for a long, long time, perhaps for ever.

Old Capulet

Mrs Capulet

Juliet led him into her room and as they embraced they lost all thought of being two separate people. Their bodies grew into one another and they became a single being, worshipping each other as the marriage words had commanded that they should, then sinking to sleep, cradled in each other's arms.

At last it was morning and time for Romeo to be up and away. Juliet begged him to stay a little longer but he knew he must be gone before the household was awake. Besides, he still had to gather his few belongings together and say good-bye to his mother and father before setting out for Mantua.

But he promised they would not be parted for long. The Montagues had good friends in Mantua and one or other of them would surely help him to find somewhere to live. Then he would send word to Juliet and she could steal away from Verona and join him, perhaps the very next week. So with many kisses they parted.

But imagine how Juliet felt when, later in the morning, her father and mother came bustling into her room to tell her that her wedding with Paris was all arranged. It would take place on the following Thursday and the Prince himself had promised to give the bride and bridegroom his blessing and to find them a tiny house in the palace grounds where they would be under his care. Old Capulet was bursting with excitement at the prospect of raising his family fortunes so high but Juliet turned pale and nearly fainted at the news. How could she tell her father that she was already married and that her husband was a Montague and the murderer of her cousin Tybalt? Where could she turn for help?

It was the nurse who came to the rescue. Why not seek advice from the old priest? After all it was he who had performed the wedding ceremony and it was in his chapel that Romeo had hidden after killing Tybalt. He was kind and wise and good. If there was any way out of the difficulty he would find it.

So, only a few hours after her marriage, Juliet went once again to the little chapel. There, standing beside the altar where she had knelt and thanked God for sending Romeo into her life and leading him to love her and marry her, she begged the priest to help her find some way of delaying her marriage to Paris until she could get a message to Romeo telling him what had happened and begging him to come at once and take her back with him to Mantua.

The old priest said he could indeed think of a way, but it would take all Juliet's courage to accept it. He possessed a rare drug which could, for the space of forty-two hours, put her into such a deep sleep that she would appear to be actually dead, her heart scarcely beating, her breathing almost stopped and her body stiff and cold. He would give her some of this drug and she must drink it on the night before the wedding which her father was now arranging. Next morning her family would think she had poisoned herself and she would be laid in the Capulet's tomb close to the bloodstained body of Tybalt which had been placed there only a few days before.

Meanwhile the priest would send a letter to Romeo telling him what had happened. Then Romeo would return at once to Verona and go straight to the Capulet tomb where he would find Juliet waiting, ready to escape with him to Mantua. There they could live openly as man and wife.

It was a hard thing to ask a young girl to do. The tomb was a huge vault carved in the solid rock and surrounded by galleries on which lay many generations of the family, not in coffins like we bury people, but dressed as they had lived, their silks and satins and brocades rotting away along with their dead bodies.

Juliet trembled at the thought of waking up in the cold vault amongst skeletons and lifeless bodies, but when she remembered that the first person she would see when she awoke would be Romeo, waiting to carry her off to Mantua, she put her fears behind her. Any risk was worth taking to escape the marriage with Paris and see her dear Romeo again.

When she got home the whole house was in a turmoil with preparations for the wedding: dresses for bride and brides-maids, rings, necklaces, satin shoes and silver girdles all being brought together for the great day and the house ablaze with flowers. Carefully she hid the drug in the drawer of her little bedside table, then went round the house pretending to enjoy the excitement, trying on her dress and her veil and her shoes, popping into the kitchen to see that the cooks were happy about the wedding breakfast, chatting with everyone so gaily that no-one suspected there could possibly be anything amiss.

Only when at last she found herself alone in her bedroom did her courage begin to fail her. What if the drug did not work?

What if by mistake it was not what the priest had promised, but a poison which would put her into a sleep from which she would never wake? What if Romeo failed to arrive in time and she was left waiting for him in the ice-cold vault without food or drink, perhaps for many days, perhaps for ever?

But then she thought of Romeo and how much she longed to be folded in his dear arms again and feel his hands on her body and his kisses on her ears and throat. Surely that was worth any danger, any risk. So, with a swift prayer to God asking him to keep Romeo safe and soon bring them together again, she swallowed the drug and lay down on her bed and fell into the deep and almost breathless sleep which the priest had promised.

All this time the nurse had been in great confusion. She knew that Juliet was already married to Romeo. She also knew that she herself had helped to bring them together and that if it were found out she would be partly to blame. So she pretended to herself that the secret marriage had never really happened or had only happened by accident. It was something that young and impulsive girls often did without thinking. No, this was the real wedding, in a fine big church with bells ringing and the organ playing and wonderful clothes and a rich and handsome bridegroom and the church full of people. A proper wedding! Juliet would soon forget Romeo and all would be well again. That was what she was feeling when she went to Juliet's room early next morning to draw the curtains and wake her young mistress.

At first she thought Juliet was simply sleeping but when she touched her and found her stiff and cold she let out a great scream and rushed from the room. Soon the whole house was roused. Juliet was dead. Now, instead of a wedding there would be a funeral and a sad procession to the Capulet's tomb.

Old Capulet, shaken with grief, ordered that Juliet should be buried in her wedding dress, with her red-gold hair flowing

loose, her hands crossed on her breast and her silver slippers on her feet.

Only when the nurse, pouring with tears, came to undress her and tenderly wash her body, did she see the silver ring hanging between her breasts and remember Romeo. Now all thoughts of the second wedding she had so much looked forward to went out of her mind. The child she was caressing with her large peasant hands was already married. Somehow her husband must see her before her body was shut away and the iron doors of the vault locked and barred. He of all people must be told what had happened. Somehow she must get a message to Mantua.

Swiftly she wrote a note: 'Come quickly—your Juliet is dead and is to be buried tomorrow'. But how could she manage to get it to Romeo? Once again she remembered the priest. Surely he would help her. Surely Romeo had told him where he could be found. She must go to the little chapel as fast as she could.

As soon as Juliet left him the old priest had sent a message to Romeo telling him that he had given Juliet the drug to save her from being forced to marry Paris, and begging him to come back to Verona at once and go straight to the Capulet's tomb where he could awaken Juliet and take her back to live with him in Mantua.

So now, when the nurse came telling him that Juliet was dead and asking him to do everything in his power to let Romeo know, the priest had to think very quickly. If he told the nurse that Juliet was only drugged and that she would soon awaken, she might well go back and tell old Capulet, who would wait till Juliet recovered and then force her to go through with the marriage to Paris just as he had planned.

So, feeling sure that his own message must have reached Mantua and that Romeo was probably already on his way back to Verona, he felt quite safe in sending the nurse's letter by the very next messenger.

But things do not always work out so easily. Life is full of mistakes, false turnings, letters that get lost or delayed, ends that never get tied up, misunderstandings. The priest's own messenger, bearing the letter telling Romeo that Juliet was only sleeping and urging him to come to Verona at once, started out on his journey, but as he approached Mantua he heard that plague had broken out in Mantua and that he would not be allowed into the city. So he thought he would wait until the plague had died down. Thus Romeo never received the old priest's message at all.

The second messenger, carrying the nurse's letter, got through to Mantua without difficulty, found Romeo at the address he had been given by the priest and gave him the nurse's letter.

When Romeo learned that Juliet was dead he was stunned. His whole world had fallen to pieces. All his hopes of a long and happy life were gone for ever. But in a flash he made up his mind. If Juliet was dead he would die too. If they could not be together in life they would be together in death. So he went to an old friend in Mantua who sold deadly poisons and bought from him enough of it to kill himself instantly, then set out for Verona as fast as he could.

No sooner had he reached Verona and gone to the churchyard than he heard someone approaching. Paris had come to lay flowers on Juliet's breast and take a last farewell. When he saw Romeo his anger flared up and he drew his sword. It was Romeo who had killed Tybalt and Paris believed it was her grief for him which had driven Juliet to take her own life. Now he would get his revenge. So the two young men fought there in the moonlight outside the vault. But as in his fight with Tybalt, Romeo was stronger and more skilful. He beat Paris backwards against the iron doors and ran his sword deep into his body, and the flowers that Paris had brought to place in Juliet's folded hands were spattered with his own blood as he fell.

As he died, Paris begged Romeo to lay him beside Juliet whom he had hoped to marry. So Romeo forced open the doors and dragged the body of Paris into the vault. Inside all was dark but soon Romeo saw Juliet lying there amidst a mountain of flowers. It was now nearly forty-two hours since she had swallowed the drug and if only he had waited a little while she would have woken to join him with a cry of joy. But he had only the nurse's letter saying that she was dead and how was he to know otherwise? Here she lay stiff and cold as a corpse. With a last cry 'Oh my love, my wife, I come to join you', he took the phial of poison from his pocket and swallowed it, then collapsed into Juliet's arms and died.

Juliet

As if by a miracle his farewell kiss and the pressure of his body against her own brought Juliet back to life. She was still cold and for a few moments she could not make out where she was or why she was still wearing her wedding dress or why Romeo was lying fully clothed at her side, apparently fast asleep. But as her eyes grew accustomed to the gloom it all came back to her. Romeo had come to take her back to Mantua, had found her sleeping and had lain down to rest until she awoke.

But when she tried to rouse him and found the phial of poison in his hand, to her horror she realised that he was dead. As she ran her hands despairingly over his body, she found a small piece of folded paper tucked into the top of his doublet. She arose and took it to the moonlight shining faintly through the half-open doors. There she unfolded it and read 'Come quickly, your Juliet is dead and is to be buried tomorrow'. Then the truth came to her like a thunderbolt. By some mischance the only word Romeo had received was this brief note telling him that she was dead and since he could not live without her he had resolved to die with her.

Heartbroken she knelt beside him, weeping bitter tears. Then, suddenly, everything became as clear to her as it had become clear to Romeo when he learnt that she was dead. If he had resolved to join her in death she could do no less for him. Swiftly she drew his dagger from its sheath, drove it into her heart and fell dying over his body.

Meanwhile the old priest began to wonder what had happened to his messenger. Why had he not brought a reply from Romeo? He went in search of him only to discover to his horror that he was still waiting at an inn half-way along the road to Mantua. Fearing the worst the priest hurried back to Verona, found the doors of the tomb open and there by the light of his lantern saw the three bodies lying side by side in death. His plan had gone wrong. Now all he could do was kneel and pray that their souls would go to paradise and that God would forgive him for the part he had played in the tragedy.

Before sunrise, news of the tragedy was all over the city, and the Capulets and Montagues, roused from sleep, thronged the churchyard, now no longer at war with each other but asking what had happened. At last came the Prince and the sorrowing parents, and the crowd parted to let them through into the tomb.

There in the dim light of the priest's lantern lay the three bodies. As he died Romeo had drawn the silver ring from Juliet's breast, the ring that had belonged to his mother, the ring which he had hoped would help to heal the quarrel between the two families, the ring with which he had wedded Juliet. As he died he had slipped it onto Juliet's finger. Now all the world could see that they were man and wife.

What he did not know, what perhaps his soul would learn in heaven, was that the quarrel was too bitter to be healed by a ring alone. It had needed Juliet's death and his own to heal it, also the death of Paris and before that the deaths of Tybalt and Mercutio, to make peace between their two families.

But now at last the quarrel was healed. The nurse and the priest told their two sad stories, and there among the shadows cast by the lantern the Prince held out his arms towards old Capulet and Montague and brought the two together. Weeping, they embraced one another and swore never again to bring bloodshed to the city of Verona. Henceforward as a memorial to their dead children, they would live in peace and harmony.

This sad story tells us how we must all learn to forgive each other however badly we feel we have been injured. Only love and understanding can rid the world of hate. It is a long, hard task but we cannot avoid it and the story of Romeo and Juliet shows us a tiny gleam of light to point the way.

Twelfth Night;

or, What You Will

The Sea Captain

Viola   Sebastian

THIS is the story of a shipwreck. It is also about a pair of twins, a boy and a girl named Sebastian and Viola—not ordinary twins but identical ones. In fact the most identical twins that ever lived. That's really why the story happened.

They were exactly the same height and they both weighed eight stone six pounds and three ounces, and they both had chestnut-coloured hair and dark green eyes with long lashes and they took the same size in shoes and stockings. And if you shut your eyes and heard them talking you wouldn't have known which was which. And they always had the same sort of haircut with tight curls clinging close round their necks. So it was impossible to tell them apart. In fact, they used to have lots of fun pretending to be each other instead of themselves. One day they even changed clothes and went to each other's schools and nobody would ever have found out except that when Viola was in the carpentry class she didn't know how to sharpen a chisel and when Sebastian was in needlework he couldn't do cross-stitch or herringbone. But they managed to pass it off and when they got home they had a good laugh about it. The only tiny difference between them was that Viola had a tiny little birthmark on her tummy, but that didn't matter because you could only see it when she was in the bath!

The story starts in a country called Illyria. You won't find it in your atlas, but if you look at a very old map you will see it just opposite Italy across the Adriatic sea. Illyria was ruled by a young Duke named Orsino. He was twenty-three years old and he was tall and good-looking and very rich and he lived in a beautiful palace not far from the sea. You would have thought he had everything a young man could possibly want. And so he had, except for one thing. He was madly in love with a young lady named Olivia who lived only a few miles away in another palace, and she wouldn't even look at him. You see her father and brother had both fallen ill and died very suddenly and she loved them both so much that she took an oath that she would never look at a man again. Certainly she would never marry. She used to go about all dressed in black with a long black veil, and, under her veil, she would often be crying when she remembered her dear father and brother.

Orsino wrote her beautiful letters but she wouldn't read them, and he sent her lovely presents, rings and bracelets and necklaces and great big boxes of chocolates, but she wouldn't even open them. And she gave orders that whenever one of his servants came to the front door her major domo—that's a sort of butler—was to send him away. In fact, he wasn't even to open the door properly but just take the chain off the hook and speak to the person through the crack. His name was Malvolio, which is an Italian word meaning 'I don't like you very much

and I hope you have bad luck'. Fancy going to bed with a name like that!

It was his job to see that the floors were properly polished, and the furniture dusted and everything kept spic and span and when Olivia had guests to stay he decided who should have the best bedroom, and he kept a book with the names of all the visitors who called, and another book with a list of all the wine in the cellar, and so on.

He was always dressed in black except for a big white collar and he was very thin on top and his back hair was brought forwards and brushed over his forehead into a curl and he kept on looking at himself in the glass and spitting on his finger to keep this curl in the right place.

He carried a long black stick with a silver knob at the top and he would point it at people and poke things with it, and his mouth was always a little bit open so that he looked as if he was just going to sneeze. And he wore artificial stuffing called shin-shapes inside his stockings because his legs were straight up and down like matchsticks and he wanted to give them a bit of roundness. And, my word, was he stuck-up! You wouldn't have liked him at all, especially when I tell you that in secret he loved Olivia as well and hoped one day he might marry her. I ask you! A major domo, thin on top and with a black curl over his forehead, more than twice her age and without any calves to his legs! Some people want their heads examined!

Now Sebastian and Viola didn't live in Illyria. They lived in Italy, at a little seaside town called Montegolfo. And one day in their summer holidays they asked their mother if they could go for a day trip along the coast in a little cargo ship. They had made friends with the captain and he had offered to take them for nothing. So their mother said yes and they promised not to get into mischief and to be back before it got dark. And she packed them up two little steak and kidney pies with two oranges each and a box of dates between them and gave them some money and away they went.

It was a glorious day. The waves sparkled in the sunshine and they had a lovely trip sitting right up in the front of the ship and letting the spray dash over them every time the ship bucketed down into a fresh wave.

But suddenly a storm came up and the ship began to toss about so much that the captain sent everybody below while the crew took in the sails and made everything secure on deck.

But it was no good. The storm got worse and the ship was tossed high up into the air and then down again with a crash. Eventually it began to break up. Viola and Sebastian were thrown into the sea and as the waves caught them they got separated. Sebastian seized a piece of the ship's mast and hung on to it. He tried to pull Viola onto it as well, but just as she stretched out her hand, a big wave caught her and carried her away. The last she saw of Sebastian, he was riding his piece of mast as if it were a pony while she went on swimming. But the waves were so strong she couldn't fight them. And she would have been drowned if the captain of the ship, who was a great broad-shouldered man and a very strong swimmer, had not grabbed her and helped her ashore.

As they stood there soaking wet and shaking the water out of their hair and eyes, Viola asked the captain the name of the country they had landed on and who was its ruler. The captain told her they had been driven across the Adriatic sea to Illyria more than a hundred miles from home and that it was ruled by a handsome young Duke named Orsino. He went on to tell her how this Duke loved Olivia but how Olivia wouldn't have anything to do with him.

Viola felt sorry for Orsino and said she would like to meet him. If the captain could help her to get some boy's clothes she could present herself at Orsino's palace and offer to be his page and sing to him and read stories and run errands and take messages to his friends. And that would give her a chance to wait and see if her dear brother had also been saved. And if, unhappily, he had been drowned and washed up on the shore, she would be there to see that he was properly buried. It would be difficult for a strange girl to be seen wandering about the town but a strange boy would not be noticed as much.

The captain said that was easy. They could go into the town and buy her a shirt and a pair of breeches and a nice doublet and he would try to find her a leather cap with a feather in it and then she would look exactly like a boy. And he felt sure Orsino would give her a job.

'Don't worry about your brother', he said. 'When the storm was at its worst I saw him tie himself to a piece of broken mast with a length of rope. You mark my words. He wasn't drowned. He'll turn up like a bad penny'.

Viola was very relieved to hear that Sebastian might still be alive and she went with the captain to get fitted out. The shop-keeper was surprised to find a girl wanting to dress up as a boy, but he hadn't sold very much that week so he gladly agreed and when they came out of the shop there she was, every inch a boy! She even stood like a boy with her feet apart and her hands stuck into her belt and said things like 'Dash my buttons!' and 'Odds bodikins!' as if she had been saying them all her life.

The only thing she had to do now was to find a boy's name. If she was to pass for a boy she couldn't go on calling herself Viola. 'My young son is called Caesario' said the captain. 'Why don't you be Caesario, too?' So they agreed she'd call herself Caesario. Then she said goodbye to the captain and set off to find Orsino's palace.

Orsino's major domo wasn't stuck up like Malvolio. His name was Benvolio, which means 'I wish you well and hope you have a jolly good time' and he took Viola straight to Orsino and said: 'This young man would like to work for you, Sir. He sings in tune and in time and he reads well and he has very good manners and we're a bit short of staff, so I think we ought to take him on.'

So Viola became Orsino's page and very soon he was telling her of his love for Olivia and how she was so cruel she wouldn't even read the letters he wrote to her but sent them all back unopened. And as for the presents, she didn't even bother to untie the ribbon.

One day when he was near to despair, Orsino said: 'Do you think you could manage to soften her heart? Would you like to try?'

'Of course,' said Viola. 'That's part of my job.'

So it was agreed that Viola should go next day to see Olivia and tell her how much Orsino loved her and try to persuade her to think of him a little more kindly. Now you must remember that although Viola was dressed as a boy and had taken a boy's name she was still very much a girl underneath, with a warm and loving heart, and during the short time she had been working for Orsino she had fallen deeply in love with him herself. And now she had to try and persuade Olivia to love him. What a mix up! Still, a page can't disobey his master, so away she went.

When she got to Olivia's palace and rang the bell, who should come to the door but that horrid old Malvolio I told you about. And, of course, he didn't want to let her in. But Olivia heard them arguing at the front door and she liked the sound of Viola's voice and told Malvolio to stop being silly. So Malvolio pulled a nasty face at Viola and let her in. Then he took her into

Viola

89

the big drawing-room where Olivia was sitting in an armchair with her veil over her face.

Somehow it seemed absurd to be talking to a person in a thick black veil so Viola asked Olivia to lift the veil and show her face. And she spoke with such grace and in such a sweet tone that Olivia couldn't help doing as she was asked. When Viola saw how lovely she was, she told her fiercely that it was wicked of her to be so hard on Orsino and not to give her heart out to him as he offered his to her.

Well, the boy's clothes suited Viola so well and she looked so handsome with her chestnut hair tumbling round her forehead and her voice sounded so brave and strong as she begged Olivia to have pity on Orsino and try to love him, that Olivia's heart began to beat faster and she felt the blood rise in her neck and cheeks. But not for love of Orsino! Suddenly, and without any warning or any chance to turn back, she had fallen desperately in love with Viola! That's just how true love happens. It isn't a thing you decide. It suddenly gets you in its power and you can't escape. Olivia could have sat listening to Viola all day—all night if necessary—she was suddenly so much in love with her.

Here indeed was a fine mix-up! Viola, pretending to be a boy called Caesario and pleading with Olivia to be kind to Orsino, when all the time she was in love with him herself! And Olivia, grieving for her dead father and brother and determined to stay unmarried till the end of her life, suddenly falling in love with Caesario, who was really a girl dressed up as a boy. This was going to take some sorting out!

When she had finished trying to persuade Olivia to love Orsino, Viola made a low bow, bade Olivia a courteous goodbye and asked Malvolio to show her out. And Malvolio did so, all too readily, for he was glad to see the back of her. But when she heard the front door shut and realised that Viola had gone, Olivia was desperate. She felt she would die if she did not see the handsome young man again, if possible the very next day. But how could she let him know? How could she get a message to him?

Suddenly she hit on an idea. When Malvolio wasn't looking she took off one of her most beautiful rings and laid it on the carpet just where Viola had been standing. Then she pretended to notice it and stooped down to pick it up. 'Look, Malvolio,' she said. 'The young man dropped this ring. Hurry after him and give it back. And tell him that if he would like to come again tomorrow he will be welcome.' And oh, how her heart was thumping and how flushed were her cheeks and how her eyes shone with pure love as she handed him the ring.

Malvolio wasn't used to hurrying but he couldn't very well disobey so he went running down the drive calling after Viola to stop. You would have cried with laughter if you had seen

him. He walked like an ostrich and when he broke into a run it was as if he was going to come apart at the joints. And you should have heard him puffing and blowing!

When at last he caught up with Viola and tried to give her back the ring, she couldn't understand it. She hadn't left a ring behind. She hadn't even been wearing a ring. So she wouldn't take it. But Malvolio put it on the end of his long black stick and laid it on the ground in front of her. Pretending he didn't want to come too close to her you see! I told you how stuck-up he was!

Maria

Sir Toby Belch

Feste

Sir Andrew

After he had gone, Viola picked the ring up and noticed that there were little hearts engraved all round the inside, with arrows through them! Then she began to realise that Olivia had fallen in love with her and she began to see just what a pickle she had got herself into by dressing up as a boy.

Now I must tell you about some of the other people in the story. Olivia had an uncle, called Sir Toby Belch, because he was always making rude noises at dinner. He was very very fat. He weighed nineteen stone seven pounds eleven ounces in his nightshirt. You see he loved eating and drinking and having a good time and playing practical jokes. He would get up at about half-past-ten and have a good solid breakfast; five fried eggs and ten rashers of bacon with lots of tea and toast and marmalade. Then at half-past-eleven he would eat a little something to fill up the corners and drink a pint or two of sack—that's a lovely sweet wine made in the Canary Islands. Then there would be lunch which was nine courses. And after lunch he would go upstairs and undress and get into bed and have what he called a snooze (sometimes as long as three hours!) then wake up nice and fresh, ready to begin eating and drinking all over again. But he was awfully kind and Olivia was very fond of him. He was like having a nice, big, lollopy sheepdog about the place.

Sir Toby had a young friend called Sir Andrew Aguecheek. That sounds rather a complicated name, but it isn't really. An ague is a sort of fever and when you have it your cheeks go rather pale, so aguecheek simply means someone with a rather white and pasty complexion. This Sir Andrew was the fourth cousin twice-removed of Sir Toby's sister-in-law's second cousin's uncle and one day Sir Toby asked him down to stay at Olivia's for a long weekend and he fell in love with Olivia and just stayed on, making himself a sort of fixture. They simply couldn't get rid of him. He was six feet nine inches tall and very thin, with a little moustache and beard and he only weighed nine stone three pounds. But he had beautiful hands and feet and he was a lovely dancer and he could make the best daisy chains in all Illyria.

Then there was Feste, which is another Italian name, meaning quick and happy and always jumping about and playing tricks. He was Olivia's jester. He was only three feet seven inches tall and he had one leg shorter than the other and a hump on his back where his mother had dropped him when he was a baby. She was trying to carry him in her arms and hang out the washing at the same time. Trying to do two things at once, you see. But Feste was very sweet and kind and he could sing and dance and do cartwheels and handstands and make jokes and tell funny stories and invent riddles. His voice was alto and he used to accompany himself on a lute, which is a very difficult instrument because sometimes it has as many as twenty strings,

so it's very hard to keep in tune. But he could keep his in tune. It seemed to come naturally to him. Also, he had perfect pitch, which is very useful. Perhaps you have perfect pitch? I wonder. You must get your singing teacher to try you out, and be sure to let me know.

Then there was Maria. She was head cook and bottlewasher. She was dark-haired and plump and when she laughed, she used to shake like a jelly and tears would run down her face. And she could make the best apple pie in all Illyria. She had learnt it from her grandmother who once went for a holiday to her sister's in Yorkshire where they make the best apple pies in all the world!

Lastly there was Fabian. He was a sort of office boy. He helped to lay the table and polish the silver, and he took the letters to the post and he had to take the five dogs for a walk every evening and see that they did their duty properly before being put down for the night. And he played the recorder and the hautbois and the viol de gamba and the bones.

Well, these five, Sir Toby, Sir Andrew, Feste, Maria and Fabian used to have midnight feasts. They would wait until Malvolio had locked the front door and seen that all the fires were out and gone to bed, then they would come creeping downstairs in their stockinged feet and go down into the cellar. And Maria would get a big venison pastie out of the larder and eight or ten roasted quails and a big piece of salt beef and a dozen herrings and two or three pounds of cheese and twenty or thirty hard-boiled eggs and some apples and pears and a few ripe peaches and a bowl of gooseberries. And Fabian would bring a firkin of sack and some tankards and Feste would carry the bowl of syllabub and the big apple pie which Maria had made specially and they would lay it all on the cellar table. Then Sir Andrew and Feste would go up the ladder and help Sir Toby through the trapdoor. He was so fat that when he was halfway through he exactly filled it. His stomach went absolutely square. But Sir Andrew and Feste pushed from the top and Fabian and Maria pulled on his feet from below and at last they got him through the hole, and his stomach gradually came back into shape again. Then they would eat and drink until they couldn't hold any more and then they would have a sing-song. Not proper singing, because Feste was the only one who could sing properly, but half-singing and half-shouting, and banging their tankards on the table.

Now one thing I forgot to tell you about Malvolio was that he had very delicate ears. They weren't very big but they were very delicate. He couldn't stand a lot of noise about the place. So, of course, Sir Toby and Sir Andrew and Maria and Feste and Fabian singing into the small hours of the morning and keeping him awake used to make him very angry and he would come downstairs in his slippers and dressing-gown and

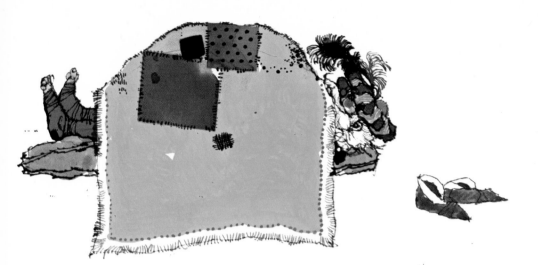

nightcap, very tired and irritable. And when he was irritable, he could be really nasty. He would give them all a long lecture, and make them tidy the place up and go off to bed. And next morning he'd split on them to Olivia and they would all get a telling off!

After the feast they knew they would never get Sir Toby back up the ladder so they used to put him to sleep on an old mattress and cover him with some old blankets and there he would lie, gently snoring till morning. One night he ate so much that next day they had to get a carpenter in to cut the trapdoor bigger, otherwise he might have had to stay in the cellar for a week or more.

Well, as you can imagine, when this boy Caesario (who wasn't really Caesario at all, but Viola in disguise) kept on coming and speaking with Olivia hour after hour on Orsino's behalf and whispering sweet nothings into her ear and making her blush, Sir Andrew began to get very jealous. He called Caesario 'a little whipper-snapper' and said he was 'poaching on other people's preserves'.

So at last Sir Toby and Maria persuaded him to send Caesario a challenge. That's a piece of paper which says 'I am going to have a fight with you and see which of us is the best. We will fight with swords, and I warn you I am pretty good at sword-fighting, so you had better look out'. He wasn't really good at sword-fighting, but, of course, Viola was afraid he might be.

Now without telling anybody Sir Toby had taken their swords to the blacksmith and got him to grind away the points and the sharp edges so that they couldn't really hurt each other. If there had been a lot of blood around it would have spoiled all the fun. Then he told Sir Andrew that Viola had once been a professional sword fighter and that she had killed three men in her fighting career. And, of course, that frightened Sir Andrew out of his wits and he said he would rather not fight someone as good as that. But Sir Toby wouldn't let him off. He made him go on with it. Viola was even more frightened than Sir Andrew because she had never used a sword at all. She hardly knew which end of a sword was which. But she had to accept the challenge. In those days if you didn't accept challenges people said you were a coward. So the time and the meeting place were fixed and everything arranged.

When Sir Toby and Maria and Feste and Fabian saw Viola standing pale and trembling waiting for the fight to begin they realised she was probably a worse fighter than Sir Andrew was,

Sir Toby Belch

Feste

Sir An

and it was very funny to see the two very frightened people with their swords drawn pretending to be brave.

At last Sir Toby and Feste said it was time to begin and they pushed the two fighters towards each other. But just as their swords met a voice shouted at them to stop, and a perfect stranger, a big strong man with a black beard, came running over to them and knocked up their swords with his own, telling Sir Andrew to stop fighting or he would kill him. Then he turned to Viola and greeted her like an old friend.

Viola was astonished because she didn't know the man. She had never set eyes on him. So she couldn't possibly greet him back. She just stood and stared at him. And then, just as this man was beginning to get angry with her for not recognising him, some guards came running down the street and arrested him and took him away. And that puzzled Viola even more.

Meanwhile (that's a very special word which means 'while all this was going on, let me tell you what was happening somewhere else') Sir Toby and Maria had played a wicked trick on Malvolio to punish him for spoiling their midnight feasts and interrupting their concerts.

Knowing that he loved Olivia and that he hoped one day he might marry her, they wrote a letter imitating Olivia's handwriting and left it lying where Malvolio would find it. They didn't actually use Olivia's name in the letter, but from the things that were said and also from the handwriting, Malvolio had no doubt at all who had written it. It said how much the writer loved and admired him and what a fine figure of a man he was and what beautiful legs he had and how well-shaped they were, especially when he wore yellow stockings criss-crossed with black ribbon.

Malvolio was overjoyed to read the letter and, of course, believed every word of it. And would you believe it, the next time he came into the drawing-room he had canary-coloured stockings on, criss-crossed with black ribbon! And he started to say such ridiculous things and pull such funny faces and blow such big kisses to Olivia that she thought he must be off his head and she had him sent to the lock-up, which was a little dark room where they put drunk people and lunatics to give them a chance to sober up and calm down. So there poor old Malvolio sat, all in the dark, in his yellow stockings and cross-garters, wondering what had happened to him. Still he deserved it for being so stuck-up and for spoiling the midnight feasts!

Now I am going to let you into a secret. You remember how Viola's brother Sebastian was last seen tying himself to a piece of ship's mast in the middle of the storm? Well, the man who stopped Viola and Sir Andrew fighting each other and had then been arrested by the guards was really the captain of a pirate ship which was also caught in the storm, and his name was Antonio. He had seen Sebastian struggling in the water and had dived in to rescue him. Then he had brought him to land. But it was very dangerous for him to be in Illyria, because some years before he had killed Orsino's brother in a sea-fight and ever since then Orsino's guards had been on the look-out for him. And if they caught him he would probably be executed.

When they came to land and had dried out their clothes, Sebastian told Antonio that his dear sister Viola had been on the ship, too, and that he must go into the town and look for her in case she had managed to get safely to land and was now looking for him.

Of course, Antonio could not go with him for fear of being arrested, so he let Sebastian go on his own, promising that they would meet later in the evening at an open space inside a little park where no one would see them. And would you believe it, this little park was really part of Olivia's estate and was the very place that Sir Toby and Maria had chosen for the fight between Sir Andrew and Viola. Being a seaman, Antonio naturally turned up in good time for his meeting with Sebastian, and when he saw Viola being attacked by Sir Andrew he thought she was Sebastian and came to her rescue. And Orsino's guards had heard the shouting and clashing of swords and had run quickly into the park and taken Antonio prisoner. So now things were even more complicated!

Sir Toby and Sir Andrew and Maria and Feste were amazed when this perfect stranger rushed up, stopped the fight and was then taken away by the guards. They had never seen him before. But when they turned to Viola to ask if she knew him, Viola was no longer there. She had put her sword back into its sheath and slipped away. She'd had enough sword-fighting to last her for the rest of her days!

But a few moments later who should come strolling into the park but Sebastian keeping the promise he had made to meet Antonio. When Sir Toby saw him he naturally thought he was Viola coming back to have another go at Sir Andrew. So he pushed Sir Andrew forward to meet him.

Sir Andrew was still very nervous, but he didn't like to show it, so he walked straight up to Sebastian and gave him a box on the ears. Sebastian was not taking an insult like that from anyone. He gave Sir Andrew a box on the ears back, a real fourpenny-one. Then he drew his sword and said: 'Come on, let's fight it out.' And a jolly good fighter he was! He soon had poor Sir Andrew down on the ground pleading for mercy. And he was so angry he might easily have done Sir Andrew real harm, but Sir Toby drew his dagger and came lumbering forward as fast as he could, roaring like a bull for Sebastian to put down his sword and leave Sir Andrew alone.

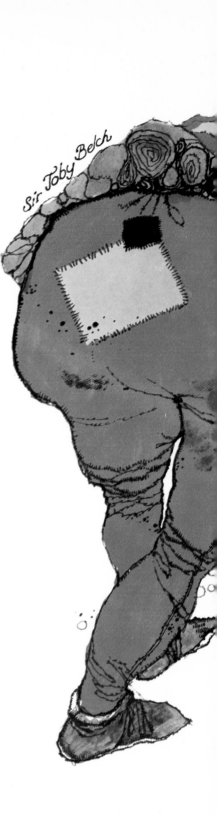

Sir Toby Belch

Now Olivia was sitting out on her verandah doing some
needlework and she heard all this shouting and came rushing
out through the kitchen garden and into the little park to see
what was happening. When she saw Sir Toby with his dagger
drawn about to attack Sebastian, she cried out to stop them
fighting. Then thinking that Sebastian was really her much-
loved page Caesario (who was really Viola!) she went up to him
and took him by the hand and led him indoors, making a big
fuss of him and apologising that her Uncle Toby had been so
rough and bad-mannered to him.

Sebastian was astonished at this beautiful young lady, whom
he had never in his life set eyes on, treating him like an old
friend and leading him into her lovely drawing-room and
making him lie down on the best couch and bringing him wine

and calling him 'her darling Caesario'. He wasn't her darling Caesario, he was Sebastian! But she was so kind and beautiful that he was quite happy to let her go on believing he was her Caesario, especially if it meant being looked after like that! The fact was that he had fallen in love with her the moment he saw her and now he couldn't take his eyes off her as she knelt beside him, holding his hand and gazing into his eyes.

Olivia in her turn was overjoyed at this great change in Caesario. Until now all her efforts to make him love her had failed. Now it seemed he had begun to love her as deeply as she loved him. And oh, how happy it made her! So happy indeed that she suggested they should send for a priest and get married without delay.

Although he had no idea who Olivia was or what he was doing in her house, Sebastian agreed. A priest was sent for and within a very few minutes the marriage was complete.

Meanwhile (there's that useful little word again!) Viola, happy to have escaped unharmed from the fight, but still wondering who it was that had saved her and why he had suddenly been arrested and taken away, returned to Orsino and was walking with him in the garden when the guards came crashing through the gate bringing with them Antonio!

When Antonio saw Viola again, walking by Orsino's side, reading to him from a book of love poetry, he flew into a rage, calling her bad names and telling Orsino how he had rescued her, pulling her out of the waves, and had taken her aboard his ship. Of course it was Sebastian he had really saved, but how was he to know? Viola had certainly been rescued by a brave sailor, but it wasn't this sailor, she was sure of that!

It was only when he actually called her Sebastian that the truth suddenly came home to Viola. This man who had interrupted her fight with Sir Andrew and who had been seized by Orsino's guards and was now calling her by her brother's name, must have saved Sebastian from the storm. So Sebastian might even now be walking about the town looking for her as she had been looking for him ever since she came to serve Orsino. She was so excited that she suddenly rushed out into the street determined to walk every inch of the town until she found her brother.

Sebastian in his turn was so happy to have found such a beautiful wife that everything else went out of his mind. Olivia asked him where he had been born and how old he was and what his father did for a living and how he came to be in Illyria. When he came to the part about the shipwreck, he suddenly remembered Antonio and how they had promised to meet. And without any warning he left the room and ran out into the street determined to find the brave friend who had saved his life. Olivia rushed to the door calling after him and telling him

Viola

to come back, but he was gone—gone, she feared, for ever. And she fainted away in the arms of her servants.

And then, turning a corner in one of the tiny side-streets of the town, Sebastian and Viola suddenly came face to face. And oh, how excited they were! They hugged and kissed and kissed and hugged and their words came tumbling out all on top of one another as they told each other their adventures since the storm. And Sebastian took Viola back to Olivia and then Viola had to confess that she was not really a boy, but Sebastian's sister. And a message was sent to Orsino and when he arrived Viola confessed to him also that she was really a girl and not a boy. Then she threw her arms around his neck and kissed him and told him how hard it had been to be his messenger to Olivia when all the time she had loved him so much herself.

Then, ashamed of being dressed as a boy and longing for Orsino to see how different she could look in a pretty dress, she hurried upstairs to see if she could find something in Olivia's wardrobe. It was the first time she had been in the upper part of the palace and, of course, she had forgotten that all Olivia's clothes were black. She went from cupboard to cupboard and all the clothes were the same. Black velvet, black silk, black satin, black taffeta, black lace. All, all black. And how could she wear black now that she was so happy?

But at last she came to a room full of the beautiful dresses Olivia had worn before her father and brother died, and oh, they were beautiful! Olive green and emerald and vermilion and saffron-coloured and pale mauve and crushed strawberry and cornflower blue, full of smocking and tucking and flouncing, some plain, some striped and some flowered, some cut high and some cut low, some for spring, some for summer, some for autumn and some for winter, a huge room-full, over a thousand dresses!

Viola wasted no time in choosing, she snatched a simple dress of rich green trimmed with gold, high in the waist and low at the neck, and luckily buttoning down the front! In a twinkling she had slipped off her doublet and breeches and was in her new outfit. A quick glance in the long mirror and she clapped her hands! She had made a good choice, she was transformed. She looked really beautiful.

When she appeared at the top of the staircase and came sailing down as if she had lived there all her life everyone cried out 'Oh how beautiful you look!' and clapped their hands.

First she kissed Olivia and asked to be forgiven for taking the dress without asking, then blushing she fell into Orsino's arms and nestled there like a bird. And suddenly Orsino was kissing her and running his fingers through her hair and everyone was crying for joy.

Of course it was the most wonderful wedding Illyria had ever seen. At first only one couple, Viola and Orsino, but then Sir Toby popped the question to Maria and she said yes. So that made two couples. Sebastian gave his sister away and Orsino gave away Maria. And there was music and dancing and feasting and Feste sang some of his most beautiful songs and made some lovely jokes and riddles and Fabian turned ten cartwheels without stopping and Sir Andrew did some wonderful card tricks and won first prize at hunt the slipper.

When the party was over Orsino and Viola called for their coach and went back to Orsino's palace which had now become Viola's new home, and as the dawn was just beginning to break over the sea they all went to bed, the lovers to lie in each others' arms, Viola in Orsino's and Olivia in Sebastian's. Maria would

Sir Toby and Maria

have lain in Sir Toby's only his stomach was so fat that she couldn't get quite near enough. But she did her best and Sir Toby promised to start slimming so she did better as time went on!

When he heard that it was his brother who had picked the quarrel, Orsino pardoned Antonio and Antonio promised to stop being a pirate. So Orsino bought him a fishing boat and he set up a shop on the beach, selling crabs, oysters and Illyrian winkles which are particularly nice.

And now you will be asking what about poor old Malvolio? Well, when they opened the lock-up and let him out he was very, very angry. After all he had been there for two days, all in the dark and without any proper food. But he soon got over it and he went away and got a job as a major domo with a nice old couple aged ninety-two and ninety-three, who were quiet and orderly and had all their meals in bed and never got drunk and went to church three times on Sunday and wouldn't have any children or animals about the house. So in the end he was happy, too, and when his employers died at the age of a hundred and six and a hundred and seven they left him their little estate and he went into partnership with Sir Andrew, growing oranges and tomatoes and radishes and parsley and pomegranates and Jerusalem artichokes, which were exported all over the world in boxes marked 'Aguecheek Brand—Finest Quality'. And they both lived to a ripe old age.

Now you have heard all about Sebastian and Viola but what about their poor mother? When they didn't get back home as they had promised, search parties were sent out to find them, but in the end they were given up for lost. Then one day there came a messenger telling all about their adventures and saying how sorry they were that in all the excitement they had forgotten to ask their mother to the wedding. But now they invited her to come over and join them in Illyria. And, of course, she packed up all her things and went over on the very next boat. And Olivia built her a little cottage at the other end of the park and she became the chief baby-sitter in Illyria! And as Viola and Olivia had four babies each she was kept pretty busy.

So you see it isn't a bad idea after all to be born an identical twin!

Gertrude

Hamlet,
Prince of Denmark

Hamlet

THE King of Denmark had just died a terrible death, infected with some rare and deadly poison that had raised ugly sores and swellings over his whole body. And no-one could tell how or why this had happened. He was still in the prime of life, scarcely fifty years old, strong and healthy and vigorous. How could this fine brave man have become so suddenly and fearfully afflicted? It was a great mystery, and many people in Denmark were troubled by it, especially when his brother Claudius suddenly seized the crown and, before the Court had time to put away their black clothes and end their mourning, married Gertrude, the dead King's widow.

Gertrude was now at the loveliest time of life, not yet forty years old, fair-skinned and dark-haired, with a beautiful mouth and a laugh like a peal of bells. She had loved the dead King and been happy with him, but he was a great soldier and scholar and statesman, and was often away from home for months on end. Even when home he was occupied with affairs of state and government, with little time for dancing and feasting and the simple pleasures which a young wife loves and so much looks forward to.

Claudius was just the opposite. He liked music and dancing and drinking and merry-making and he had a fine sense of humour. He made everyone around him feel light-hearted and gay. So it was natural that Gertrude should be attracted to him and enjoy being with him, and not unnatural, when her husband died, that she should marry him. Somehow they suited each other. But many people thought she had married again far too soon after her husband's death and they disliked the idea that she should have married her dead husband's brother, especially as there were still grave doubts as to how her first husband had died.

Now the dead King had a son named Hamlet; young, handsome, sensitive, courteous and brave. He had loved and admired his father and was deeply grieved when he died and even more deeply grieved when his mother married Claudius. So even when the whole Court had gone back into ordinary clothes, Hamlet stayed in his black suit, mourning his dead father and wondering how his mother could ever have come to marry a man as shallow and worldly as Claudius, after having been for so long the faithful wife of his brave and noble father. He was also greatly puzzled to know how his father had come to die so suddenly and mysteriously. He was soon to learn.

The royal castle was at Elsinore, a vast rock overhanging the sea on Denmark's northern coast. And one bitter winter's night, not long after the funeral of the dead King, the two guards stationed on the castle battlements, along with Horatio Hamlet's best friend, had a strange experience. A ghostly figure, dressed in full armour and looking for all the world like the

The Ghost

dead King, came gliding silently out of the mist, then melted
away into the face of the rock on which the castle stood.

They challenged it but it made no answer, and this puzzled
and frightened them.

And then suddenly, without warning, even as they stood
talking together, there came a sudden blast of wind and a low
roll of thunder, and there it was again, in a swirl of mist, the
same tall ghostly figure, handsome and bearded, in full armour
but with the face-guard of its helmet raised to show the piercing
gaze of its eyes.

Gathering all his courage, Horatio spoke, asking if it really
was the dead King's ghost and if so why it had returned to walk

the earth at dead of night. His voice rang out sharp and clear in the frosty air: 'By Heaven, I charge thee, speak!'

But the ghost made no reply. For a moment it paused and opened its mouth as if about to speak. Then it strode on. They tried to stand in its way and, more from nervousness than anger, even struck at it with their swords. But the swords slashed the empty air. The ghost was gone. One moment it was there within a few feet of them, the next moment it had vanished, leaving Horatio and the two guards trembling with fear and wonder.

But now at least they were sure it was the spirit of the dead King, for it had come so close they could see every detail of its mouth and the way its beard was cut and the eyes which seemed to be pleading for help.

In the end they decided to tell Hamlet. Surely the one person the ghost would speak to would be its own son! Hamlet was still mourning, he was still in the depths of sorrow, but it was their duty to tell him. He must come on guard with them the next night and put the matter to the test.

So they told Hamlet all that had happened and the next night he joined them on the watchtower. And sure enough the ghost appeared again, this time not striding past but stopping quite close and gazing with sorrowful eyes upon its son. In a wild voice Hamlet spoke to it, calling it 'King! Father! Royal Dane!' and asking why it had come back from the grave and why it was walking fully armed along the castle battlements. Once again the ghost made no answer, but with a kingly sweep of its arm, beckoned Hamlet to follow it to another part of the battlements, away from where the others were standing. Then it moved on.

Hamlet

Guard

Horatio

At first Horatio and the two guards tried to prevent Hamlet from following. They feared the ghost might tempt him over the edge of the castle walls, to be dashed to pieces on the rocks below. They even tried to stop him by force, gripping him by the arms and shoulders. But Hamlet tore himself free and followed where the ghost was pointing to a sheltered corner of the watchtower, hidden from view. There the ghost had stopped and very soon Hamlet came up to it, amazed to find himself standing close to a being that belonged not to the world of the living but of the dead. Now he was to know how and why his father had died. For in a low hoarse whisper the ghost at last began to speak.

Yes, he said, he was indeed the spirit of Hamlet's father and his death had not been a natural one. He had been murdered by Claudius his own brother, who had then made himself king and married Hamlet's mother.

109

The King of Denmark

He described how one autumn afternoon, after a hard morning's work on affairs of state, he had been sleeping in his orchard, lying as he usually did on a simple couch brought out from the palace, and how Claudius had stolen quietly into the orchard with a flask of deadly poison and had poured some of it into his ear. The poison had run through the winding passages into his brain, then spread over his whole body until he was in a raging fever. The courtiers carried him into the royal bedroom and the doctors did all they could to save him but he died in indescribable pain. And Claudius told everybody that it was a poisonous snake which had caused his death.

Then, most terrible of all, the ghost said that Hamlet must there and then swear a solemn oath to kill Claudius as a punishment for having killed him.

Now I must tell you that in olden times people believed that if you died without being given a chance to say your prayers and ask forgiveness for all the wrong things you had done in life, you would go to a place full of fire and torment where you might have to stay for hundreds of years until your bad deeds were burnt away and you could pass on to the place of light and peace and blessedness, where God dwelt with his angels. And as Claudius had murdered Hamlet's father while he was still asleep, without giving him a chance to say his prayers, that was where he now was, in the region of blazing fire, and that was why he had come begging Hamlet to murder Claudius in return for Claudius having murdered him.

Hamlet's father was really a fine and noble man who had knelt and prayed every night of his life and who really deserved everlasting happiness when he died. But now he was living in this place of punishment and he felt angry and bitter, not only that Claudius had murdered him but that after only a very few weeks he had taken Gertrude as his wife.

If he had been given the chance to pray before dying it would have been different. But coming from that fearful place and knowing that he must return there at cock-crow, his mind still contained evil thoughts and one of the most evil thoughts in the world is the idea of revenge, of getting one's own back, of hurting the person who has hurt oneself. And most terrible of all, not doing it oneself but getting someone else to do it, in this case his own son. But Hamlet had loved his father and now that he heard this account of his death, hated his uncle so much that he swore to obey. Everything else should be set aside until the dreadful duty of killing Claudius was accomplished.

And then the first faint streaks of morning began to lighten the east. It was time for the ghost to say farewell. So, with a last long piercing gaze into Hamlet's eyes, it disappeared, leaving him alone on the battlements, trembling at the thought of what he had promised to do, burning with hatred and stricken with grief that his mother could ever have brought herself to marry such a man as Claudius.

Now think what a terrible position Hamlet was in! He was young and gentle and sensitive, and his heart was always offering up words of praise and thanks for the beauty of the earth and for all living things.

Yet now he had taken a solemn oath to kill a fellow human being, wicked it is true, but made like himself, of flesh and bone and blood, a piece of marvellous machinery created in the likeness of God himself. And this thought put his mind into a terrible confusion and even as he stood there in the cold morning air he began to realise how hard it was going to be when it came to doing the fearful deed his dead father had commanded him to do. And cold as it was, the sweat poured down his face as he made his way back to where Horatio and the two guards, Marcellus and Bernardo, were waiting.

There he made them take an oath just as solemn as the one his father had laid on him. They must swear never to breathe a word of what they had seen and heard that night to a single soul, and if they saw him behaving strangely and wildly about the palace, pretending that he had become unbalanced, they would take no notice but treat him as if he were quite normal.

For he had already decided that the only way to hide his hatred of Claudius and keep secret the fact that he was really planning to kill him, was to pretend that his brain had become unhinged, that he was no longer his old clear-thinking self, but half-mad with sorrow for his dead father. And Horatio and Marcellus and Bernardo swore to do as they were bidden.

Now Claudius had an old courtier named Polonius, who gave him advice and managed many of the country's affairs. He was quite clever and experienced, but very pompous and stuck-up and I am sure you would have hated him.

This Polonius had a son Laertes, the same age as Hamlet. Also a beautiful daughter named Ophelia. Hamlet and Laertes liked each other. They used to play at sword-fighting together and all the courtiers would crowd round to watch them and make bets on which one would be the winner. And Ophelia would give Hamlet a ring or a silk handkerchief for luck because she loved him and hoped that one day she might marry him. And Hamlet loved her as much as she loved him, and wrote little poems telling her how beautiful she was.

But Polonius was angry when he saw that Ophelia and Hamlet had fallen in love and that they were sending letters to each other. He reminded Ophelia that Hamlet was a prince and would one day marry a princess, not a silly young girl like her. She should not smile at him so much and if he sent more letters she must show them to her father and he would put a stop to this love-letter-writing once and for all.

Polonius

Ophelia

113

Although it made her very unhappy, Ophelia obeyed her father and began to treat Hamlet coldly, avoiding him as much as she could and if by chance they happened to find themselves together, trying never to meet his eyes with her own.

It made Hamlet sorrowful to think that Ophelia whom he loved and trusted, seemed now to have turned against him. She and Horatio had been the only two people he could open his heart to and now she had suddenly become cold and distant, just when he most needed her. For he had suddenly begun to doubt whether the ghost he had seen and spoken to was really the ghost of his dead father. What if it had been an evil spirit sent by the Devil to trick him? How could he find out? How could he prove it? How could he be sure?

And even if he were sure, even if the story it had told of his father's death were proved beyond any doubt, he still had to decide when to kill Claudius and how. Should he tempt him to walk along the castle walls, then suddenly push him over the edge on to the rocks below? Or put poison into his wine? Or wait for him in a dark corridor and stab him as he passed?

Hamlet was so puzzled and bewildered by all these questions that he more than once thought of committing suicide. Surely if life was such a torture it would be better to end it once and for all. But then he thought that death might be only another kind of sleep, full of ugly dreams, and that inside those dreams there might be other dreams, on and on and on, never ending, dreams from which he would never wake.

So he wandered about the castle trying to make up his mind, watching and waiting and being carefully watched by Claudius and Polonius. Then quite suddenly something happened which helped him to decide. A troupe of actors arrived at the Court asking if they could give a performance in the great hall of the castle. They were left to discuss with Hamlet the various details; where the stage should be placed, what time the performance should begin and what play they should present.

When they told Hamlet they had recently been performing a play called 'The Murder of King Gonzago', he suddenly had an idea that he could use this play to prove beyond doubt whether the story the ghost had told him was true or not. All he needed was that the actors should put into their performance a short scene which he would write at once and which he felt sure would greatly improve the play and please the King.

They readily agreed, and Hamlet wrote a scene in which a murderer entered an orchard and poured poison into King Gonzago's ear, just as the ghost said Claudius had done to him. If Claudius turned pale or looked frightened when he saw this part of the play, Hamlet would be sure at last that the ghost had been telling him the truth and that it really was the spirit of his father and not an evil one. Once he was really sure, it would put an end to his hesitation and would strengthen his will to kill Claudius.

Before the performance began the great hall was blazing with torches and there was a huge log fire burning, but when Claudius and Gertrude came in to take their seats Hamlet had the torches put out, so that only the stage was fully lit. Claudius was in a good temper. He had had an excellent dinner with plenty of wine and was looking forward to the play. He sat with Gertrude's hand in his, and the courtiers grouped themselves around, some standing, some sitting, some lying on cushions close to the stage. Hamlet found a place from which he could watch Claudius and notice any change in his expression without Claudius knowing he was being watched. He had written the

Hamlet

Claudius

extra scene, given it to the leading player and made sure he understood it properly. Now he waited to see what effect it would have.

The first part of the play went very well, but when King Gonzago lay down on his couch to sleep, Claudius frowned and moved uneasily in his chair. Then, when the murderer came on with his flask of poison and poured some of it into the sleeping King's ear, Claudius sprang to his feet, overturning his chair and crying 'Lights! Lights! Lights!', rushed from the hall followed by the Queen, leaving the play half-finished and everything in confusion.

The only one who was not confused was Hamlet. He was so excited he could hardly contain himself. At last he had proof. At last he was sure. Claudius had given himself away. The story the ghost had told him was true. Hamlet felt as if a great weight had been lifted from his shoulders.

Now it was no longer a question of whether he should kill Claudius or not, but only of when and where and how, and that would be easy compared with the torture of uncertainty he had endured ever since that night on the castle battlements when the ghost had told him his strange and ugly story.

Claudius was now quite frightened. Yet he was still not sure how much Hamlet knew about his father's death. The only person who could be trusted to find out was Gertrude. She must send for him to come at once to her room, then question him so cleverly that he would give himself away. And Polonius must hide behind the curtains and listen to their conversation and report every word that was said. Then, one way or another, Claudius would know whether Hamlet knew the truth.

Meanwhile the thought of his past wickedness had struck him so sharply that he suddenly felt the need to ask God's forgiveness. So he left Gertrude and Polonius and went into the tiny chapel which had not been used since the death of Hamlet's father. There he fell on his knees in prayer.

When Hamlet heard that his mother wanted to see him he at once made his way up the stone staircase and along the gallery that led to her room, past the chapel where Claudius had gone to pray. The door was ajar and there was Claudius kneeling at the altar, his hands clasped and his eyes raised to Heaven. Now was Hamlet's chance. He could steal up behind Claudius and stab him as he prayed. Then he could rest content. At last he would have kept his promise.

He pushed the door of the chapel a little further open and slipped inside, then crept silently up to Claudius and stood behind him. His sword made no sound as he drew it from its sheath. Claudius went on praying as Hamlet looked down at him, choosing where to strike his blow. It was all too easy. He would drive the blade down past the side of the neck straight into the heart like a bull-fighter killing a bull. Claudius would fall forwards and die instantly there on the altar steps, without uttering a cry.

But once again Hamlet hesitated. Here was Claudius on his knees asking God to forgive him for all the wicked things he had done in life. If he had given Hamlet's father a chance to pray his spirit would not now be in the place of horror, waiting for its sins to be burnt and purged away. If Claudius died while he was praying, his spirit would go to the place of everlasting peace instead of to the long, long punishment it had deserved. Surely it would be better to wait until he was drunk or lying or swearing or taking God's name in vain, then stab him quickly before he could even say 'God forgive me'.

So Hamlet slipped his sword quietly back into its sheath and tip-toed out of the chapel leaving Claudius on his knees, unaware that he had been so close to death.

As soon as Hamlet entered his mother's room she began to scold him, telling him how angry he had made Claudius by allowing the actors to perform such a play. Surely he realised it would suggest that his father had not died from a snake-bite as everybody had been told, but that someone had murdered him as Gonzago was murdered in the play, and that people might even believe that the murderer had been Claudius.

At this Hamlet, who was now sure that Claudius certainly was his father's murderer, flew into a rage and screamed at his mother, gripping her by the shoulders and shaking her. How could she ever have married a creature like Claudius? How could she ever have stooped so low?

His wild looks and angry words so terrified the Queen that she cried out for help. And Polonius, hiding behind the curtains and fearing that Hamlet might be doing her some injury, echoed her cry. Hearing this, and thinking that the King must have come swiftly from the chapel into the Queen's room to listen to their conversation, Hamlet suddenly made the decision he had been struggling to make for so long. He drew his sword and stabbed viciously through the curtains at the place where he saw them moving. He felt his sword enter the body hidden behind them, but when he drew the curtains back he saw that it was not Claudius he had killed but Polonius.

When Claudius heard that Hamlet had killed Polonius he realised that his own life was now in great danger, and that he must act quickly if he wanted to stay alive, for he knew that Hamlet had meant to kill him. So he made a very clever plan. He pretended that the people of Denmark were angry that Polonius had been killed and that they were demanding that Hamlet should be severely punished. Hamlet must leave Denmark with all speed and not return until the people's anger had died down. A ship was sailing for England the very next

day and two of Hamlet's old schoolfellows, Rosencrantz and Guildenstern, were sailing with her, carrying an important letter from Claudius to the English King.

Hamlet realised that Claudius would now be more closely guarded than ever before and that he must wait some time for another chance to kill him. Besides, after the shock of killing Polonius, he wanted a chance to calm his mind. So, although he had no great feeling of friendliness for Rosencrantz and Guildenstern, he went aboard the ship that very night, without knowing that the letter they were taking to the King of England demanded that he should be put to death the moment he set foot on English soil.

One night, when the ship was well on its way, Hamlet lay tossing in his bunk, unable to sleep. He had a strange feeling that although Rosencrantz and Guildenstern were so friendly on the surface, their charming smiles were false and that his life was in great danger. So he slipped out of his bunk and, wrapping a warm cloak round him, crept bare-foot along the passageway that led to the cabin where Rosencrantz and Guildenstern were sleeping. There he found the letter they were delivering to the King of England and stole quietly back to his own cabin to read it by the dim light of a lantern. His fears had been true. As soon as the ship reached England his head was to be struck off. The smiles and friendliness of Rosencrantz and Guildenstern were all a pretence. They had plotted with Claudius to have him murdered.

Swiftly he took his pen and wrote another letter, ordering that Rosencrantz and Guildenstern should be put to death instead of himself, then sealed it with his dead father's ring which he always carried with him. The letter ordering his own death he tore into tiny pieces and threw overboard, then returned to Rosencrantz and Guildenstern's cabin and put the new letter back where he had found the old one. And all the time Rosencrantz and Guildenstern slept soundly. Their trick had been discovered. It was they who would be put to death, not Hamlet.

Next day they met a pirate ship and fought a battle with her. They managed to fight the pirates off, but the pirate ship came so close that Hamlet jumped on board her and stayed there. He told the pirates who he was and how Claudius had planned to have him murdered as soon as he reached England. He also showed them his father's ring with the royal seal.

Hamlet was so brave and courteous and the story he told was obviously so true that the pirates accepted him as one of themselves and promised to take him back to Denmark as soon as possible. They would land him by night a few miles along the coast from Elsinore. And they were as good as their word. They brought their ship close to land, then rowed Hamlet ashore in a small boat, running it up the beach so that he could step out dry-footed, then they clasped his hand and wished him good fortune and rowed back again.

The pathway from the shore back to the castle ran past the royal graveyard where for centuries the kings and queens and noblemen of Denmark had been buried. As Hamlet drew near he heard low voices and saw a simple procession led by a priest coming slowly towards him.

He moved into the shadows and stood as still as a stone waiting for it to pass. As it drew near he saw two bearers

The Pirate ship

carrying the body of a girl, wrapped in a white shroud, her hands clasped together on her breast, holding a spray of wild flowers, her long hair falling back over the bier. Suddenly, by the pale light of the moon, Hamlet saw that the dead girl was Ophelia. She had loved Hamlet deeply and truly, and even when she could no longer see him or write to him, had gone on loving him. But when she heard that he had killed her father she had gone out of her mind and drowned herself. Now she was being buried.

Following the body were Claudius and Gertrude and Ophelia's brother Laertes, with Horatio and a few other mourners. They passed within a few feet of Hamlet but he was hidden in the shadows and no-one saw him. So the procession passed through the gateway into the graveyard and Hamlet fell on his knees in the shadow of the wall and asked God to let Ophelia's dear soul rest in peace. And he wept for sorrow, remembering all the happy hours they had spent together, and begged forgiveness for having killed her father.

When Claudius heard that Hamlet had returned to Elsinore he realised that his plot had failed and that he must quickly think of another one. For he well knew that the stab through the curtains which had killed Polonius had really been meant for him and that the next time he might not be so lucky.

The plan he now thought of was a very clever one. He remembered that in the old days Hamlet and Laertes had often had friendly sword fights, showing off their skill before the Court, always, of course, using swords with blunted points so

as never to wound each other. He also knew that Laertes now hated Hamlet for having killed his father and driven his sister to drown herself. He would persuade Laertes to pretend that he understood why all this had happened, that it made no difference to his friendship with Hamlet and that he would like to fight with him again, to see if they were still as skilful as they used to be. But Claudius would give Laertes a sword with a razor-sharp point and would dip it into a deadly poison, so that if he gave Hamlet only the slightest scratch it would kill him.

Claudius would also put poison into the flask of wine that always stood on the table close to the throne. He knew that even in fun, sword-fighting was hard work and that Hamlet would want to quench his thirst between the rounds. So if Laertes failed to wound him with the poisoned sword, Hamlet would die from drinking the poisoned wine.

The fight took place in the great hall where the players had performed 'The Murder of Gonzago', and the whole Court, including Horatio, turned out to watch. They knew that Hamlet and Laertes were more or less equally matched, and that they could expect a good fight. Claudius and Gertrude sat side by side on their thrones, raised up a little above all the others, and a courtier named Osric was chosen to act as referee. It was agreed that there should be five rounds and whichever one managed to touch the other one first with the tip of his sword should be considered to have won that particular round and would receive one point, and the first one to get three points would be the winner.

The swords were lying on a table close to where Claudius was sitting and no-one noticed that one of their points had been carefully sharpened, and, of course, no-one knew that the point had been dipped in poison and no-one except Claudius and Laertes knew that it was going to be a fight to the death and not a friendly one at all.

Hamlet and Laertes wore light soft-soled shoes and tight closely-buttoned jackets, and when they threw off their cloaks they looked very fine: young and well-shaped and both very handsome; Hamlet dark-haired with deep-set black eyes, Laertes like his sister, blue-eyed and fair. They advanced towards Claudius and Gertrude and having bowed to the whole assembly, shook hands. Then Claudius handed each one his sword, being careful to give Laertes the poisoned one. They swished them through the air, testing them for weight and springiness. Then Osric called them to the centre of the hall and gave the signal for the fight to begin and the two young men began to move cautiously round each other, their soft shoes padding on the floor and their swords meeting every now and again for a few seconds as they tried to press each other off balance and gain the advantage.

Laertes

After a few minutes Hamlet broke through Laertes' guard and touched him on the arm with the blunted tip of his sword, so Osric declared that the first round had gone to Hamlet. After taking a short rest they started the second round and this one was much harder. They moved to and fro across the floor, first one pressing forward, then the other, and the courtiers applauded whenever, by strength or cleverness or swift-footedness, they avoided being touched. Their swords pressed against each other as each one tried to force his opponent off balance.

Then Hamlet broke through Laertes' guard again and touched him on the chest and all the courtiers applauded. Hamlet now had two points, Laertes none.

Hamlet was fighting better than he had ever done before and he was smiling when his mother took a towel and wiped the sweat from his brow. But when she offered him some wine to refresh himself, he refused. He would drink later. Never mind, said the Queen, she would take some wine herself. And before Claudius had time to stop her she had filled a goblet from the poisoned flask and almost drained it to the bottom.

Claudius would have prevented her but he knew that if he snatched the goblet from her hand the whole Court would realise that the wine was poisoned. So, apart from the look of terror that crossed his face, he made no move. Only beads of sweat stood on his brow and he felt his heart knock at his ribs as if it was about to burst.

It was now the third round. Laertes was fighting furiously and Hamlet began to suspect that the fight was not meant to be as friendly as he had anticipated. First he drove Laertes back, then Laertes drove him back, and the courtiers held their breath as the two fighters pressed each other to and fro, and all you could hear was their feet padding on the floor and their hard breathing and the occasional clink of steel on steel as their swords touched each other.

At last Laertes broke through Hamlet's guard and scratched him on the arm with the poisoned blade. It was only a tiny cut but Hamlet felt the sting and suddenly realised that the point of Laertes' sword had been sharpened and dipped in poison and

Hamlet

that Claudius must have persuaded Laertes to try and kill him.

Hamlet was now wild with anger. He felt the poison running into his blood and knew it must soon reach his heart and kill him. Indeed he had only a few more minutes to live. How could he keep his promise to his father's ghost in so short a time?

For a brief moment he thought of rushing at Claudius and stabbing him, there on his throne. But then he remembered that his sword was the blunted one. It could never be used for killing. Besides Osric had already called for the next round to begin, so for the moment all his concentration was on the fight. How could he gain the advantage? Suddenly he had an idea. With a fierce slash he knocked the poisoned sword out of Laertes' hand, sprang forward and held it firmly to the floor with his foot, then picked it up and gave Laertes his own. Hamlet now had the poisoned sword and Laertes the blunted one.

Claudius saw Hamlet change the swords and had just sprung to his feet to stop the fight when the Queen gave a wild cry and slid from her throne to the floor, groaning and clutching her sides as she felt the poisoned wine burning in her blood.

Claudius called to the ladies-in-waiting to help lift her up. She was already close to death, but gathering up all her strength she managed to cry out a warning to Hamlet. 'The wine,' she cried, 'the wine is poisoned.' Then she collapsed and died.

Hamlet heard the warning but he did not dare to break off the fight. He was being pressed too closely. But at last he got the upper hand and forced Laertes back amongst the ring of spectators. Then, with a final swift pass he ran his sword into Laertes' throat. The blade went right through his neck and out at the back and Laertes fell to his knees in agony as he felt the poison creeping through his veins. He had just enough strength left to pull Hamlet down beside him, to confess that he had plotted with Claudius and to ask Hamlet to forgive him. Then he also died.

As Hamlet staggered to his feet Claudius was still holding the Queen in his arms. Hamlet rushed at him and tore her from his grasp, then ran his sword, still dripping with Laertes' blood, straight into his heart. Then he snatched the flask of wine and,

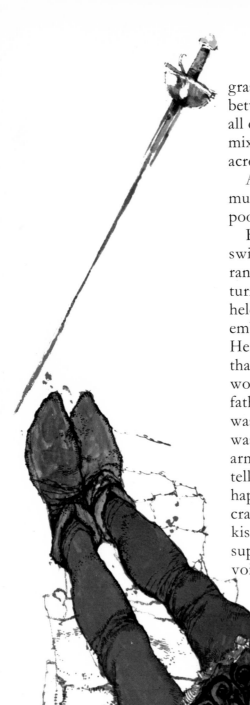

grasping Claudius by the shoulders, forced the silver rim between his teeth until they parted and the deadly wine gushed all over his face and into his mouth. Claudius screamed. Wine mixed with blood poured from his mouth and he fell headlong across the floor, gasping in his death agony.

At last Hamlet had kept his promise. The man who had murdered his father was now dead, sprawled on the floor in a pool of his own blood.

But Hamlet was now near his own end. His sight was swimming and he could scarcely stand. His dear friend Horatio ran out from amongst the spectators to hold him up and as he turned over in the agony of death, Hamlet saw his dead mother, held by her waiting-women, her arms stretched out as if to embrace him. He had lost his father and his beloved Ophelia. He had fought his way through all the dangers and treacheries that had faced him. Now he was about to die and there was the woman who had given him birth. It was in her body that his father had planted the seed that had grown into their child. It was in her arms that he had snuggled as a tiny child whenever he was sleepy or frightened. Now he felt a deep desire to feel those arms around him once again. In a whisper he begged Horatio to tell the people of Denmark the truth about all that had happened, then he dropped to his knees and half stumbling, half crawling, fell into his mother's arms, and there, pressing a last kiss on her lips, died. And from among the rafters that supported the roof there came soft music and the sound of voices, as if angels were singing him to his last sleep.

Claudius

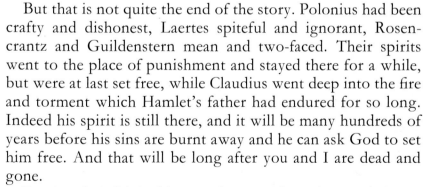
Hamlet

Gertrude

But that is not quite the end of the story. Polonius had been crafty and dishonest, Laertes spiteful and ignorant, Rosencrantz and Guildenstern mean and two-faced. Their spirits went to the place of punishment and stayed there for a while, but were at last set free, while Claudius went deep into the fire and torment which Hamlet's father had endured for so long. Indeed his spirit is still there, and it will be many hundreds of years before his sins are burnt away and he can ask God to set him free. And that will be long after you and I are dead and gone.

But Hamlet's life had been so brave and good, he had always been so humble and considerate, he had thought of the world and all its wonders with such reverence and delight that his life had been a living prayer. So his spirit went at once to the place of light and peace where Ophelia's spirit was waiting to receive him. And through his suffering he was allowed to rescue his father's spirit from its prison house and unite it with his mother's. She had been lazy and careless but never wicked, and in dying her only thoughts had been for her son and for God's mercy. So the four of them were joined together and are still joined and will never be separated.